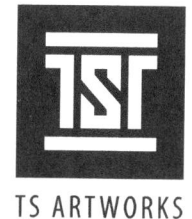

TS ARTWORKS

Floral Designs
Coloring Book

Art and Design by
Taranjit S Layal

© 2018 Taranjit S Layal

All rights reserved. No part of this publication may be reproduced or transmitted in any form or by any means, electronic or mechanical, including photocopy, recording or any information storage and retrieval system, without permission in writing from the author.

www.tsartworks.com

Floral Designs Coloring Book by TS Artworks

www.tsartworks.com

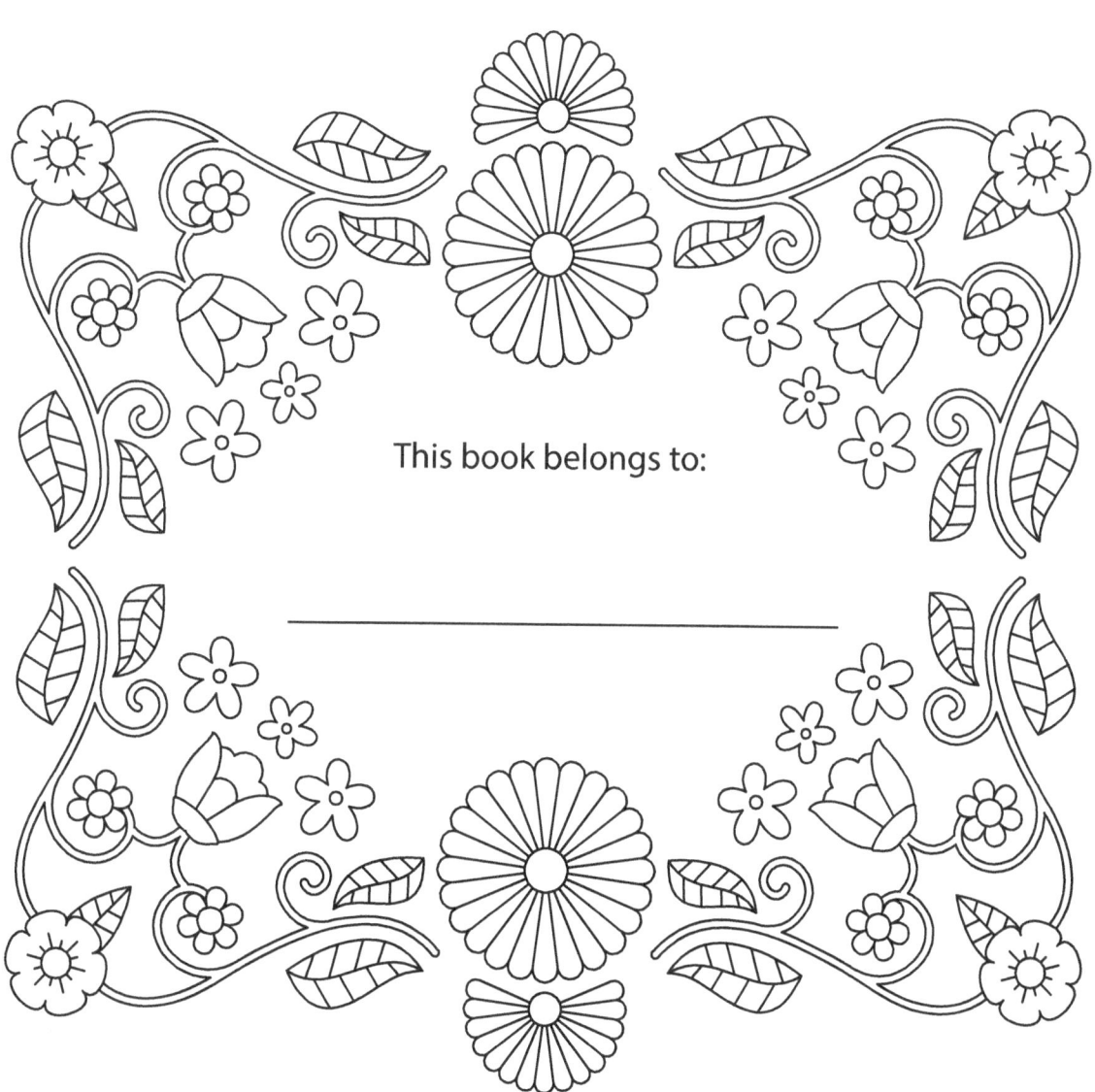

This book belongs to:

_____

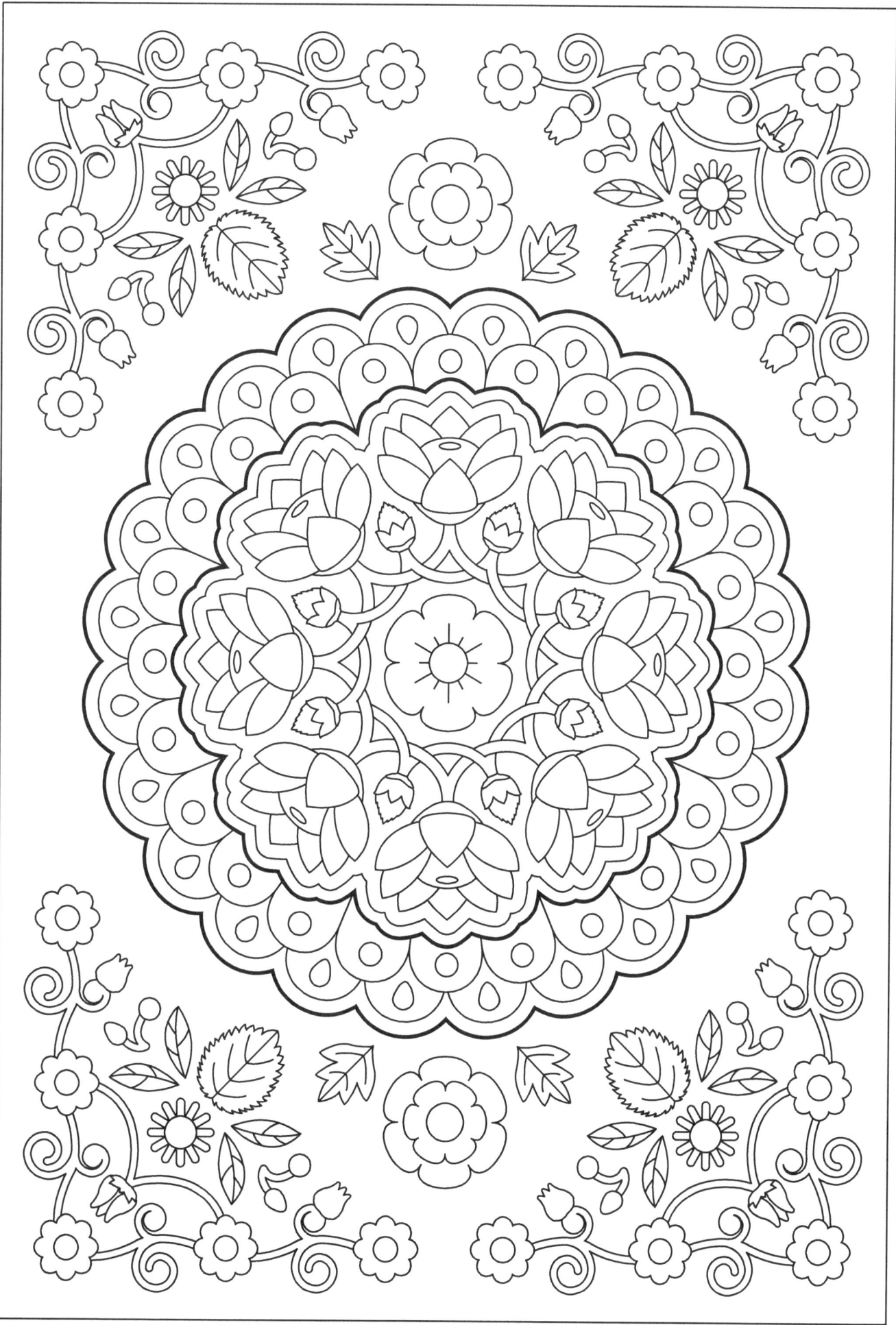

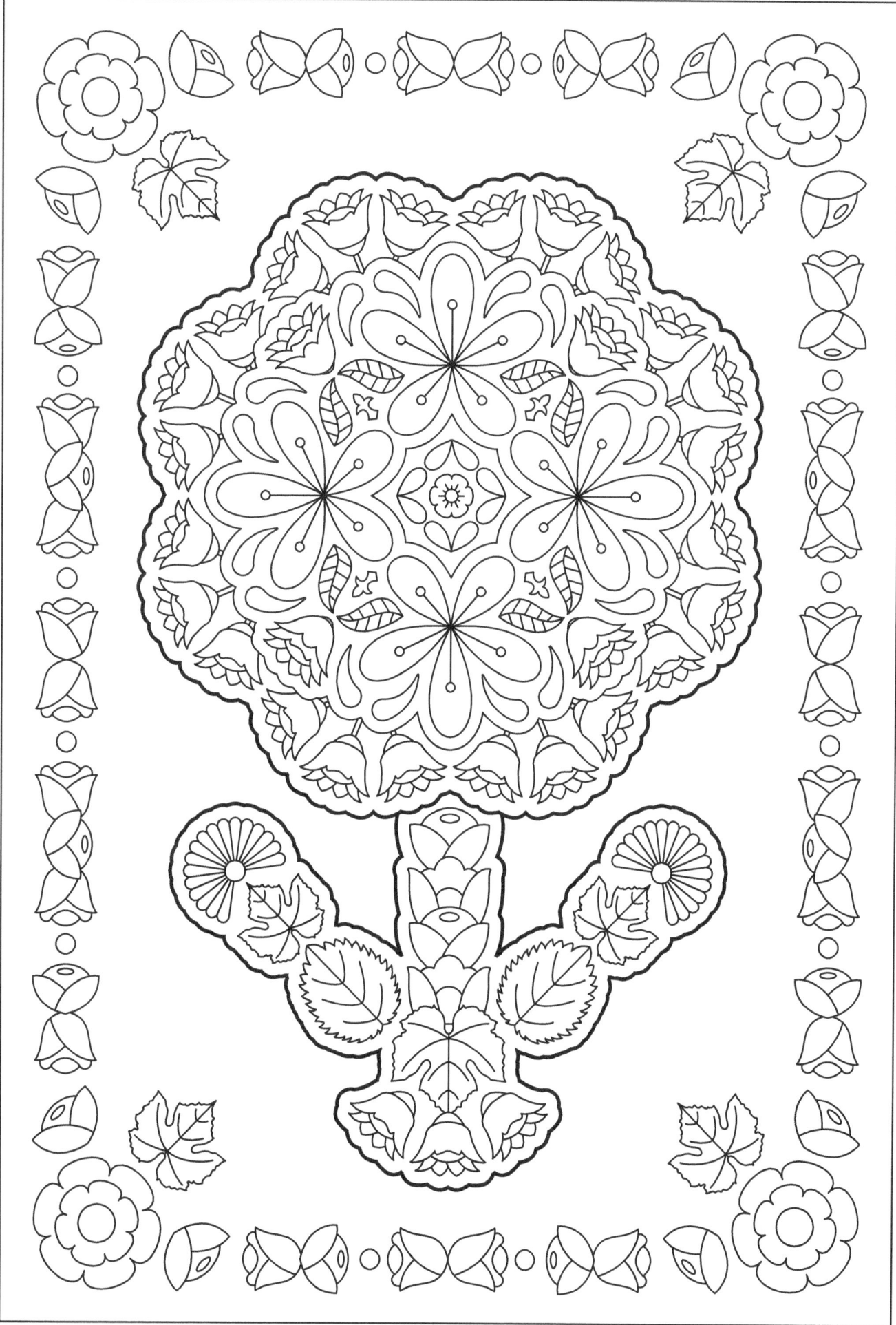

Floral Designs Coloring Book by TS Artworks

www.tsartworks.com

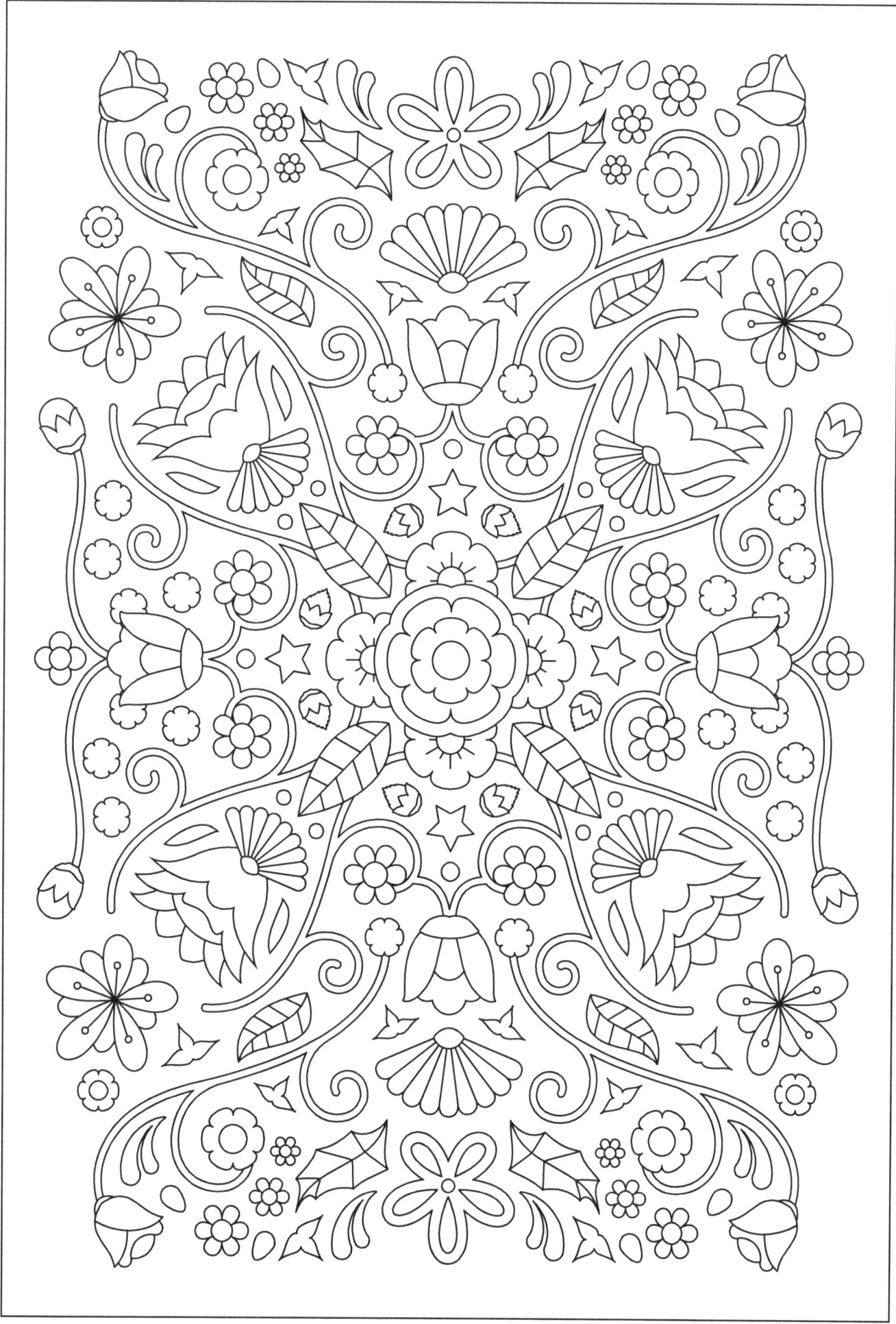

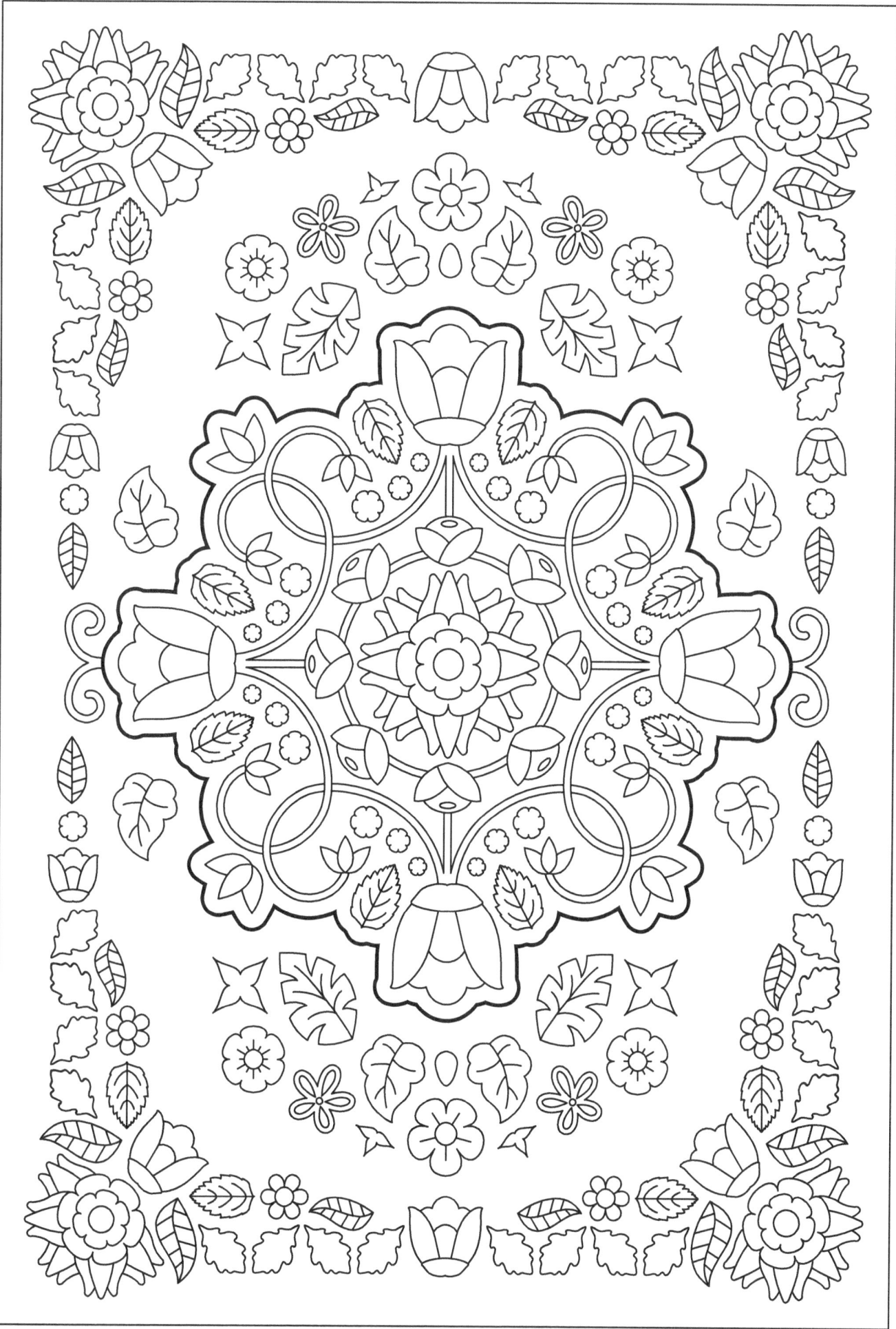

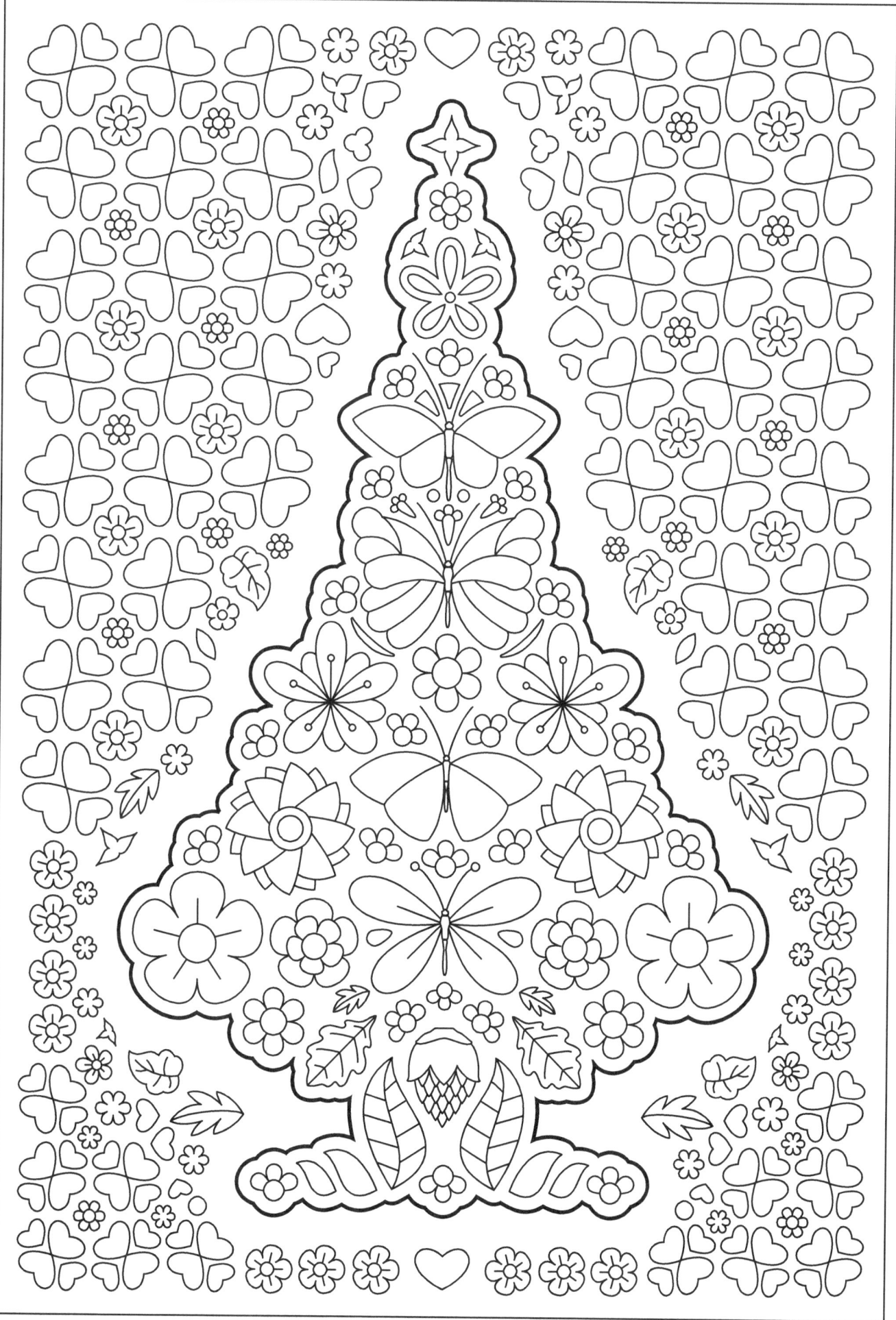

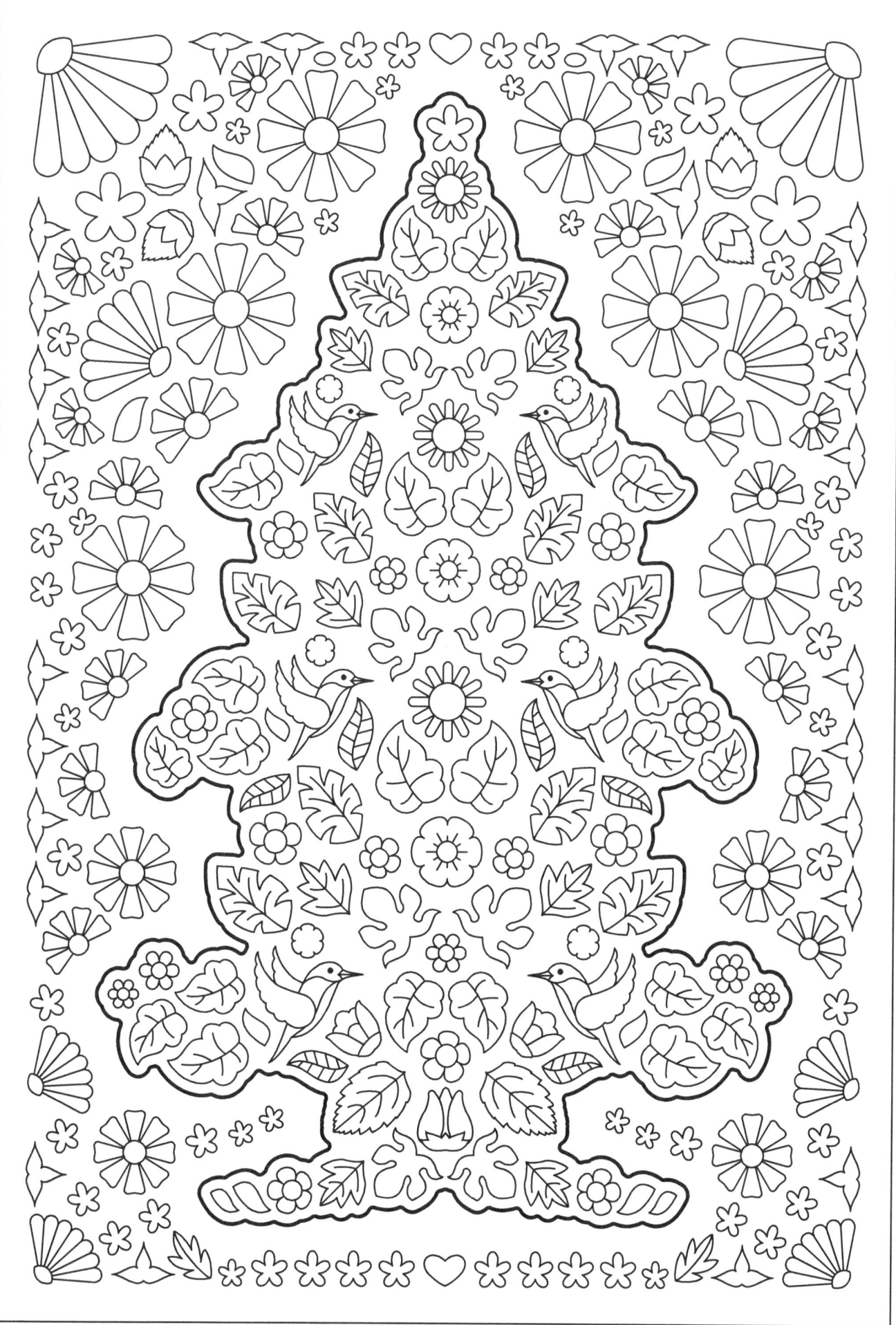

Floral Designs Coloring Book by TS Artworks

www.tsartworks.com

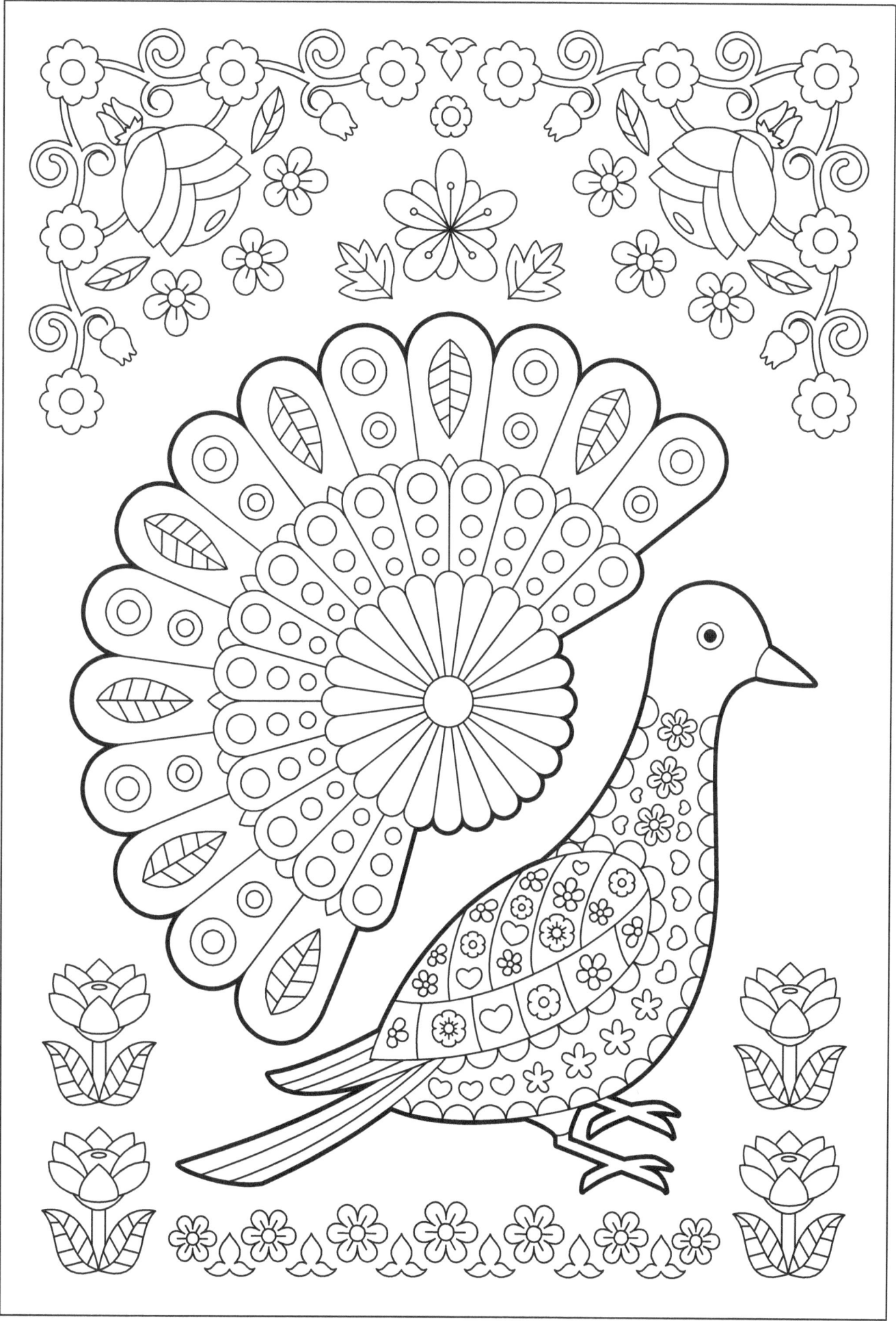

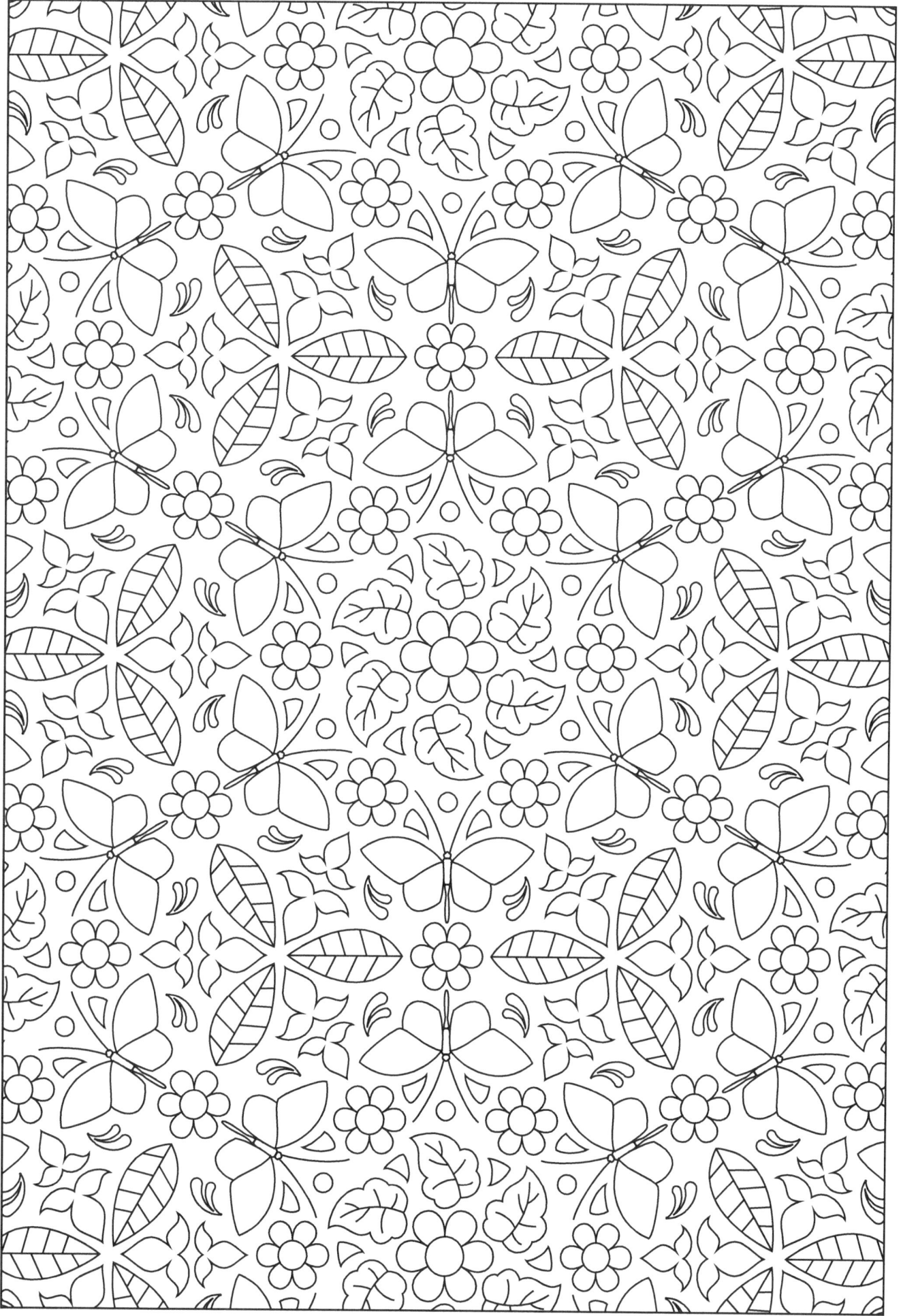

Floral Designs Coloring Book by TS Artworks

www.tsartworks.com

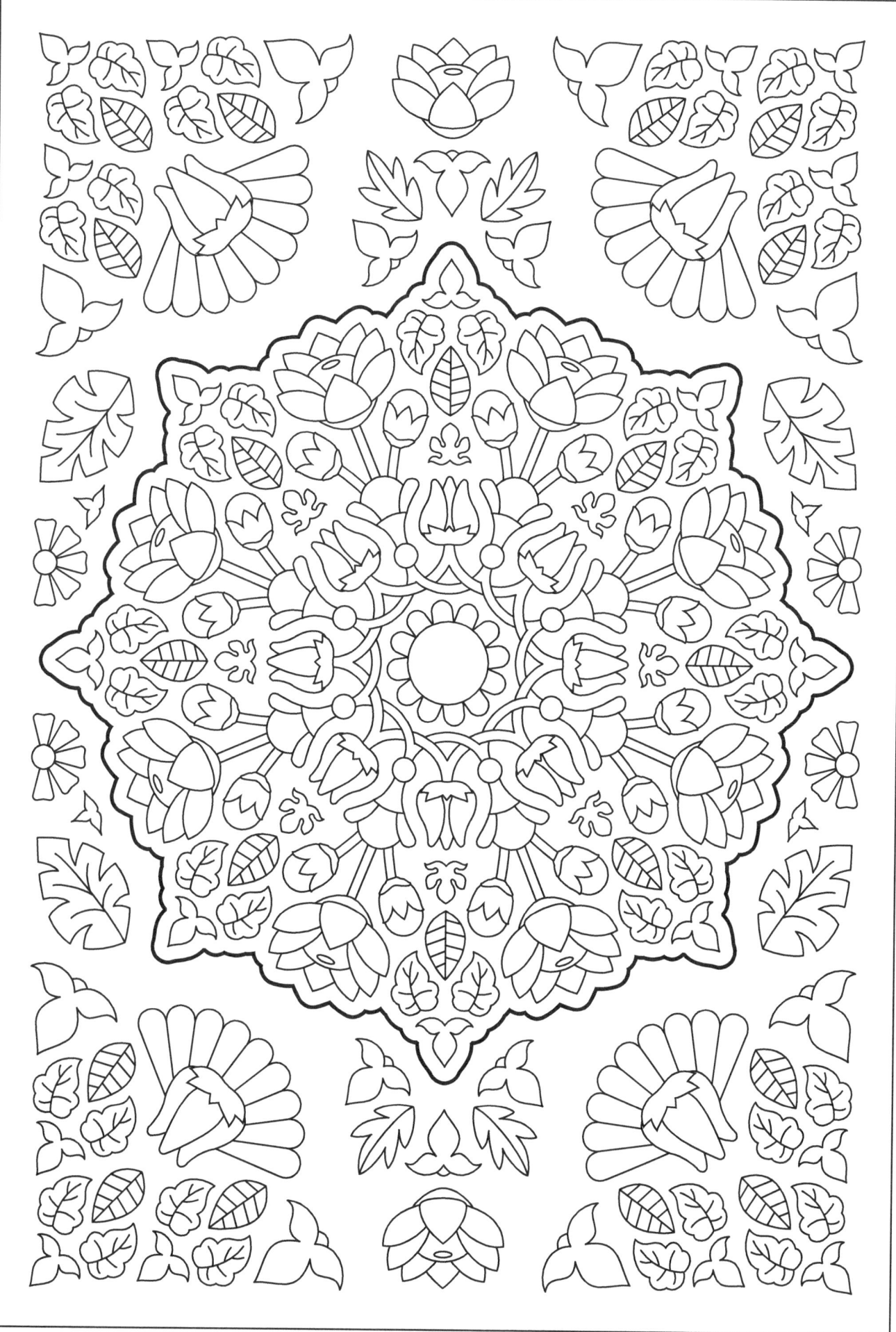

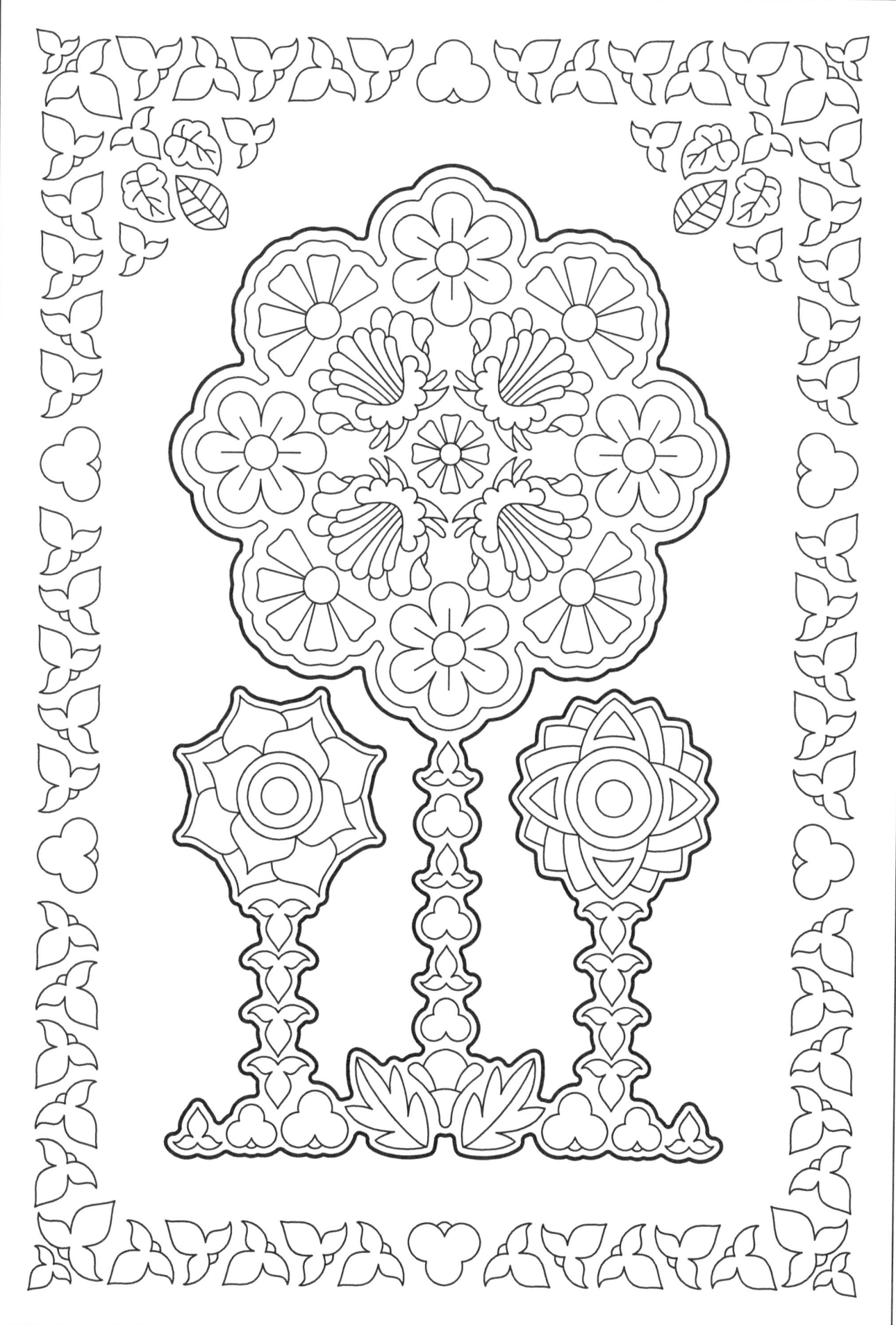

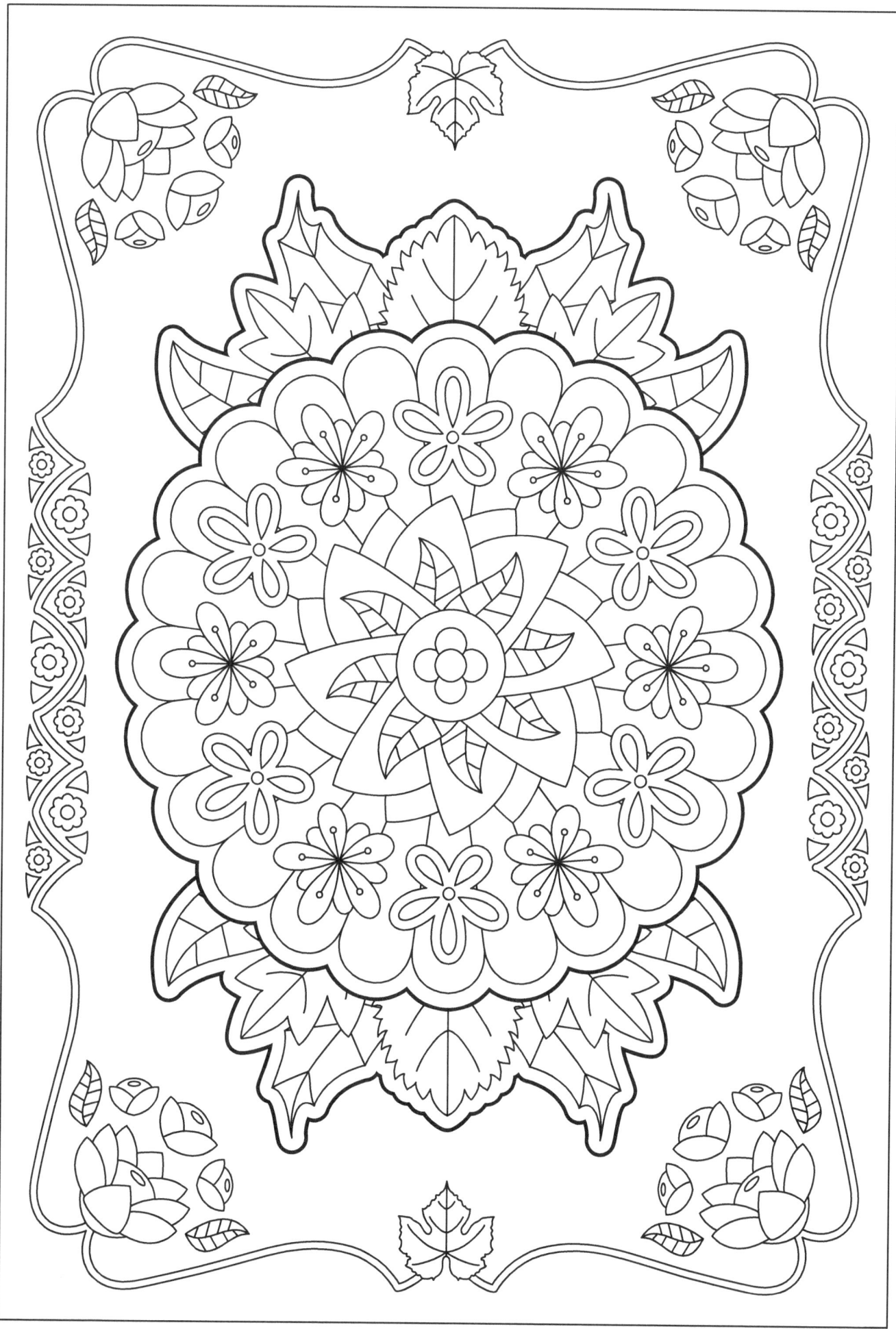

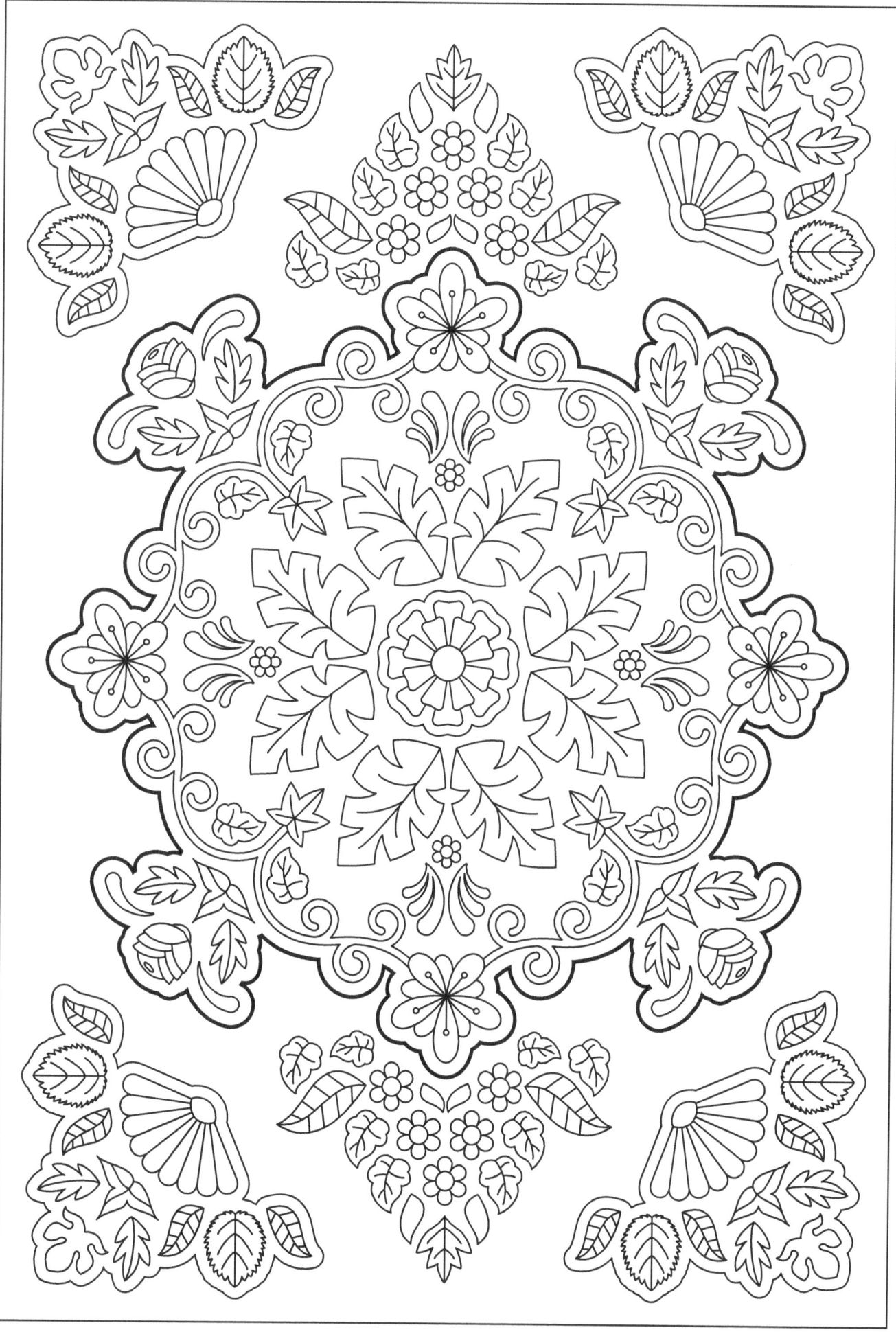

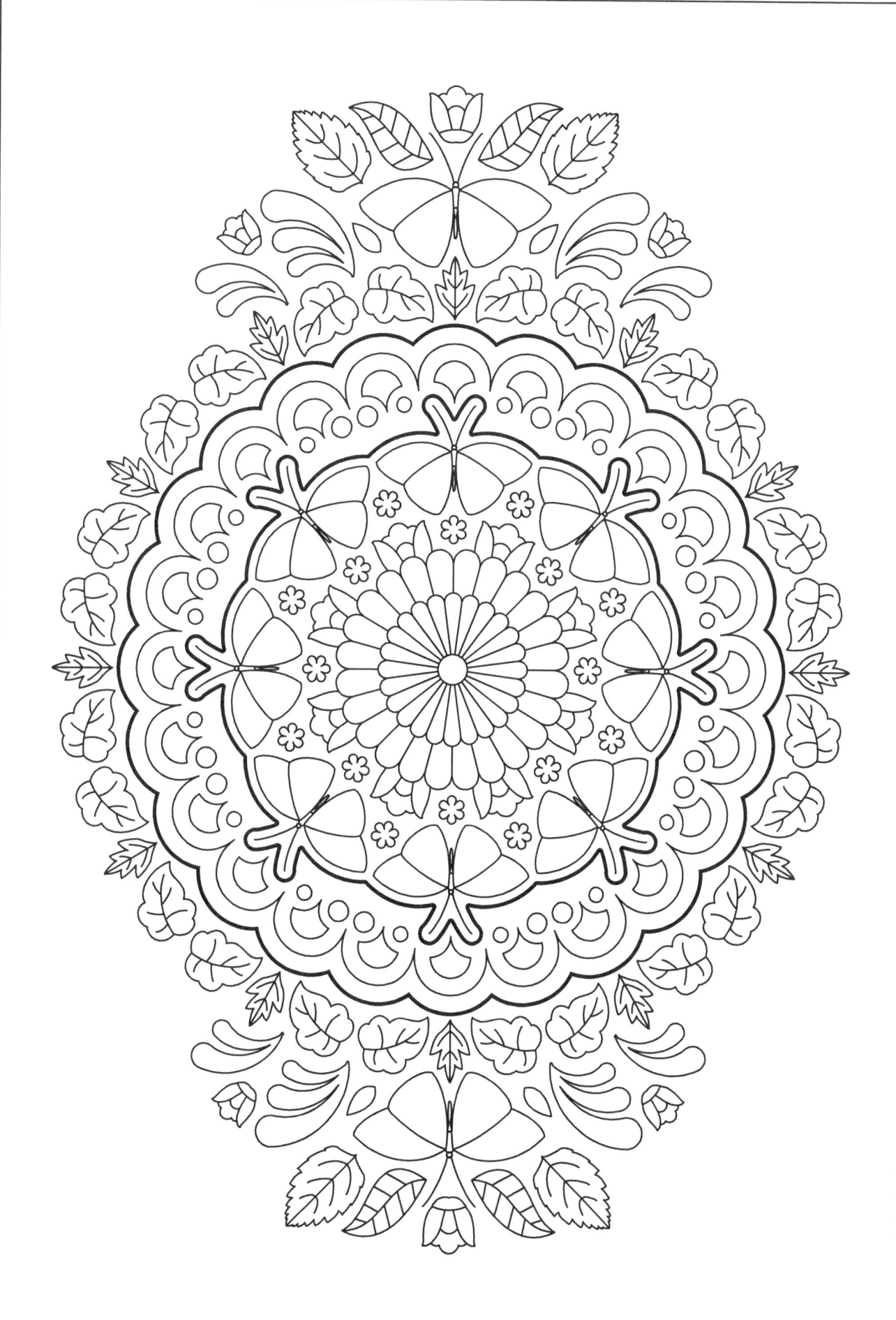

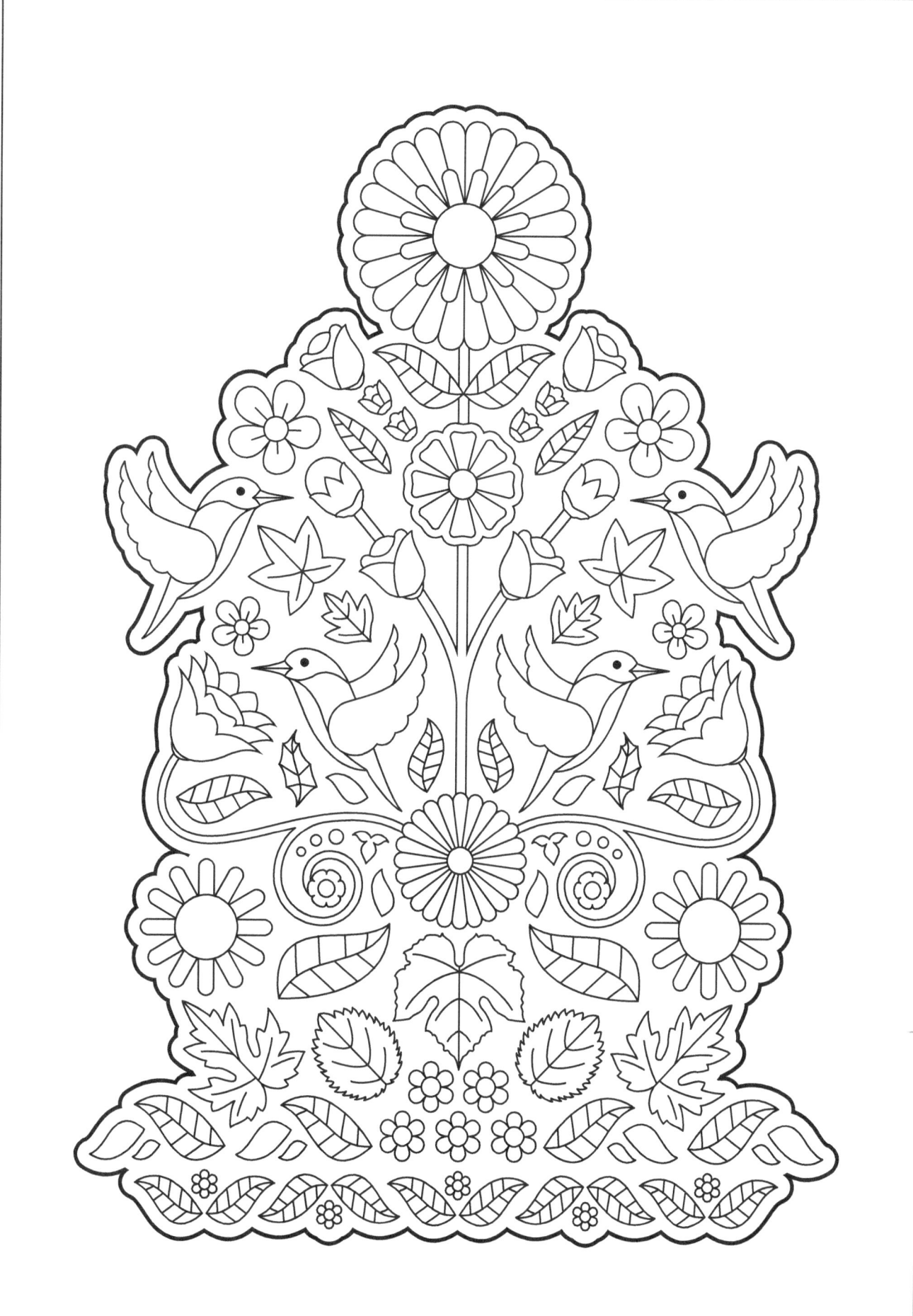

Floral Designs Coloring Book by TS Artworks

Floral Designs Coloring Book by TS Artworks

www.tsartworks.com

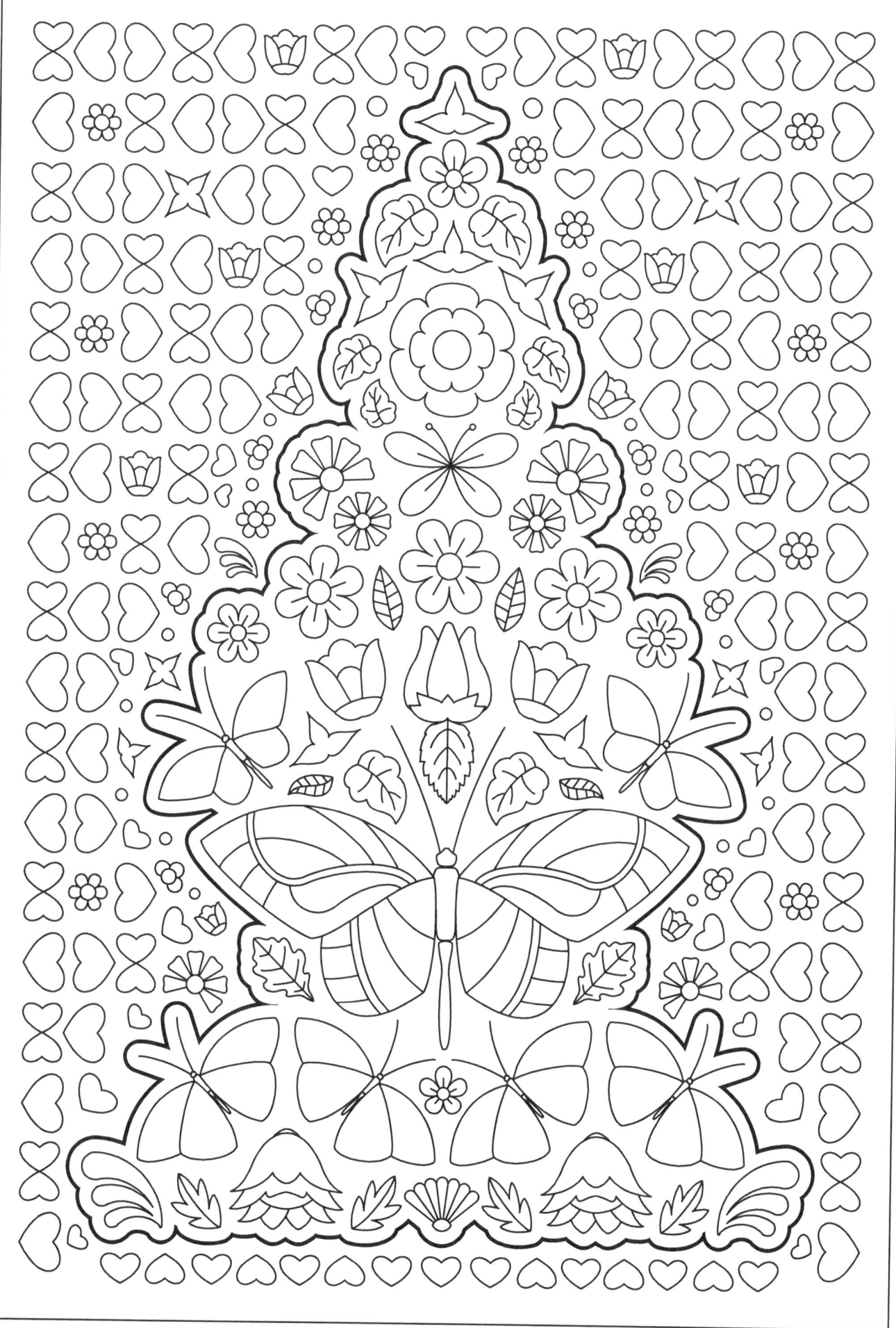

Floral Designs Coloring Book by TS Artworks

www.tsartworks.com

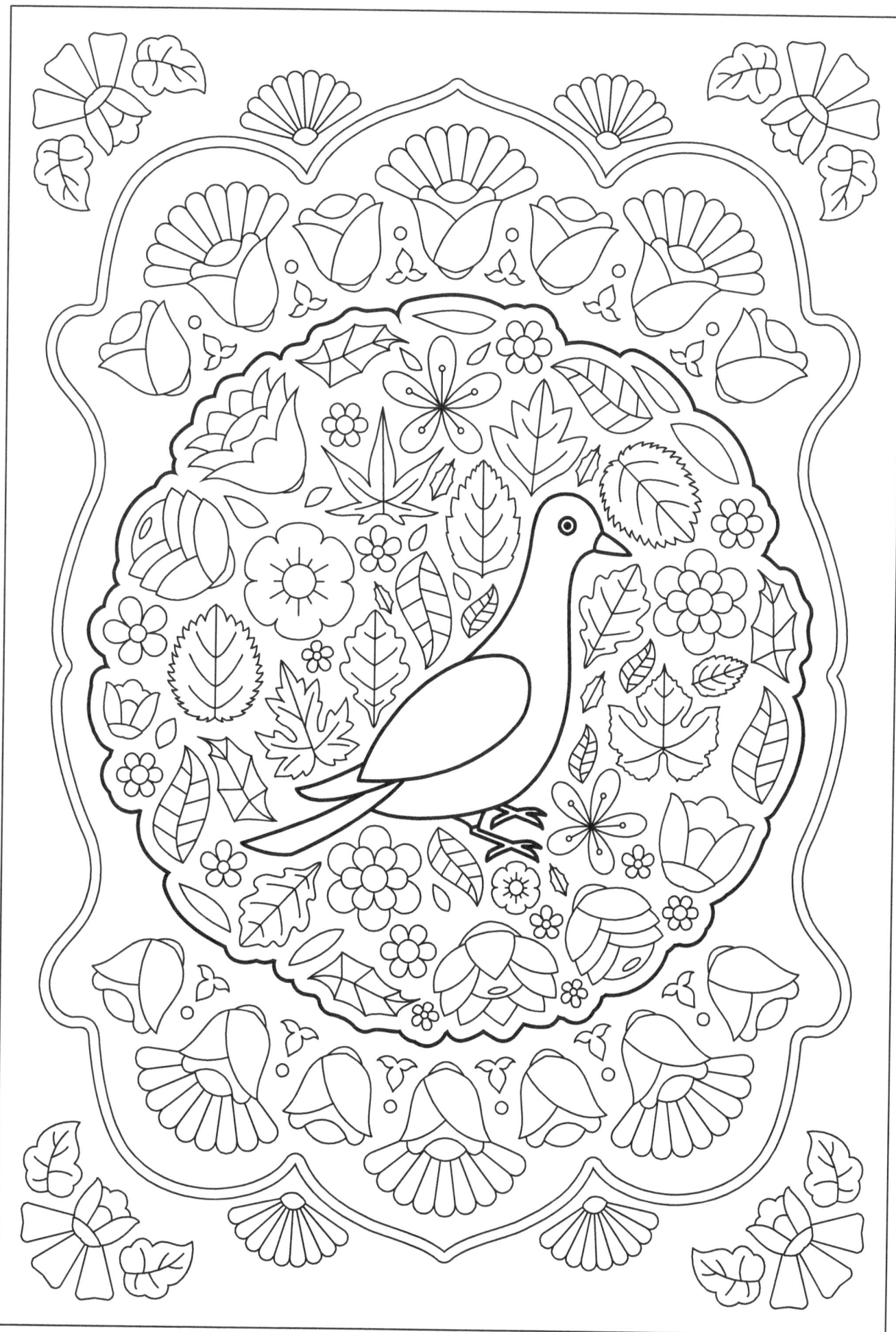

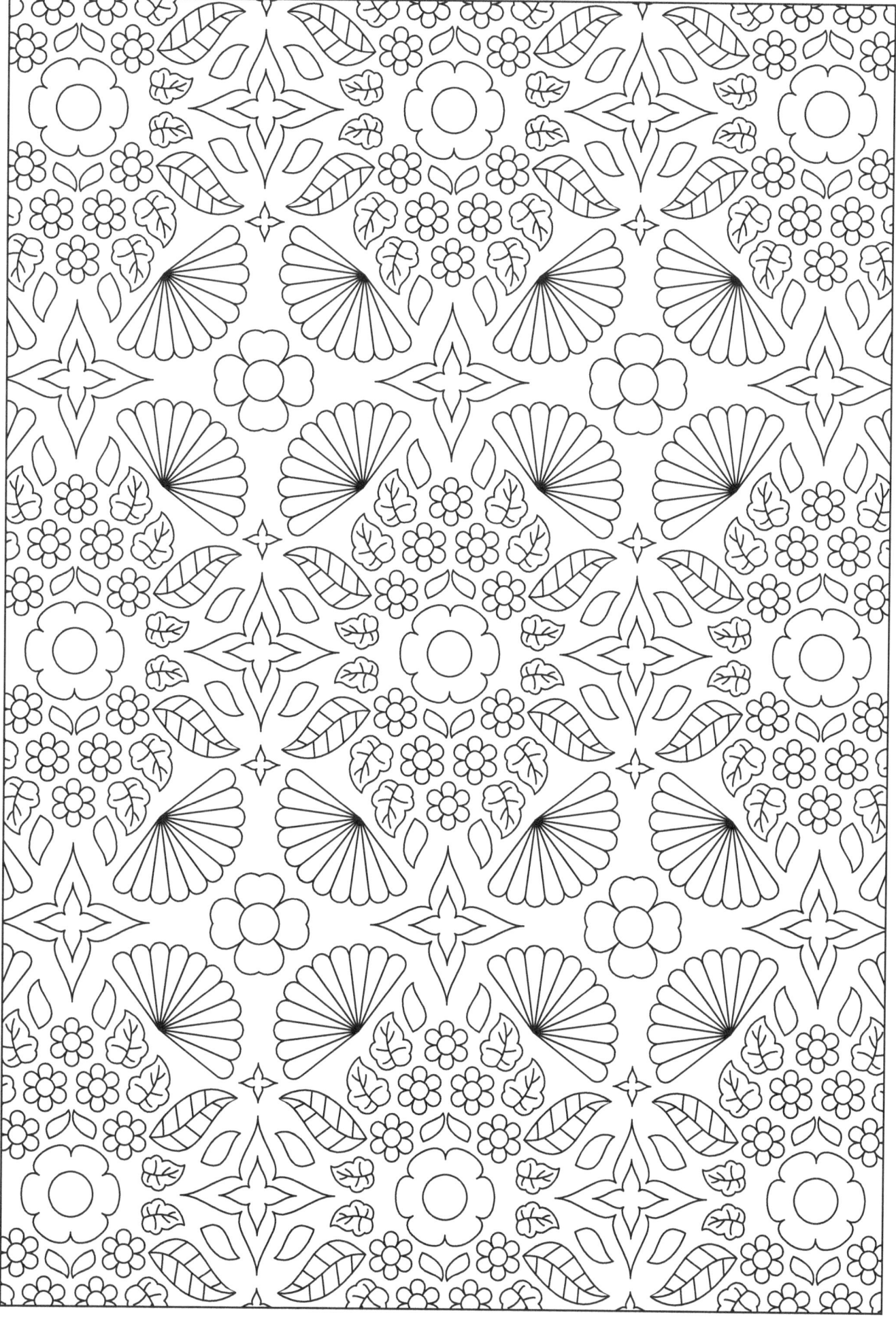

Floral Designs Coloring Book by TS Artworks

www.tsartworks.com

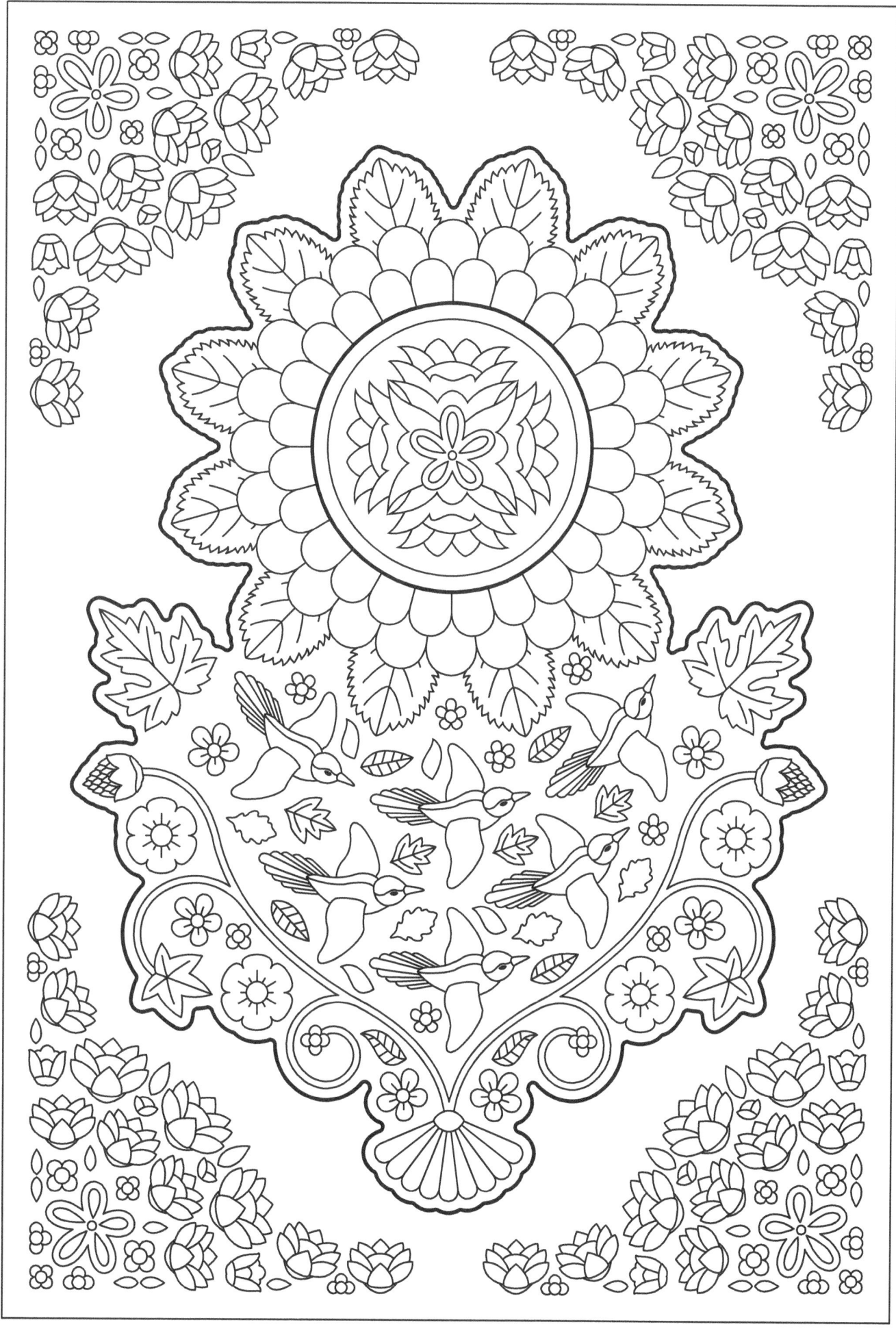

Floral Designs Coloring Book by TS Artworks

www.tsartworks.com

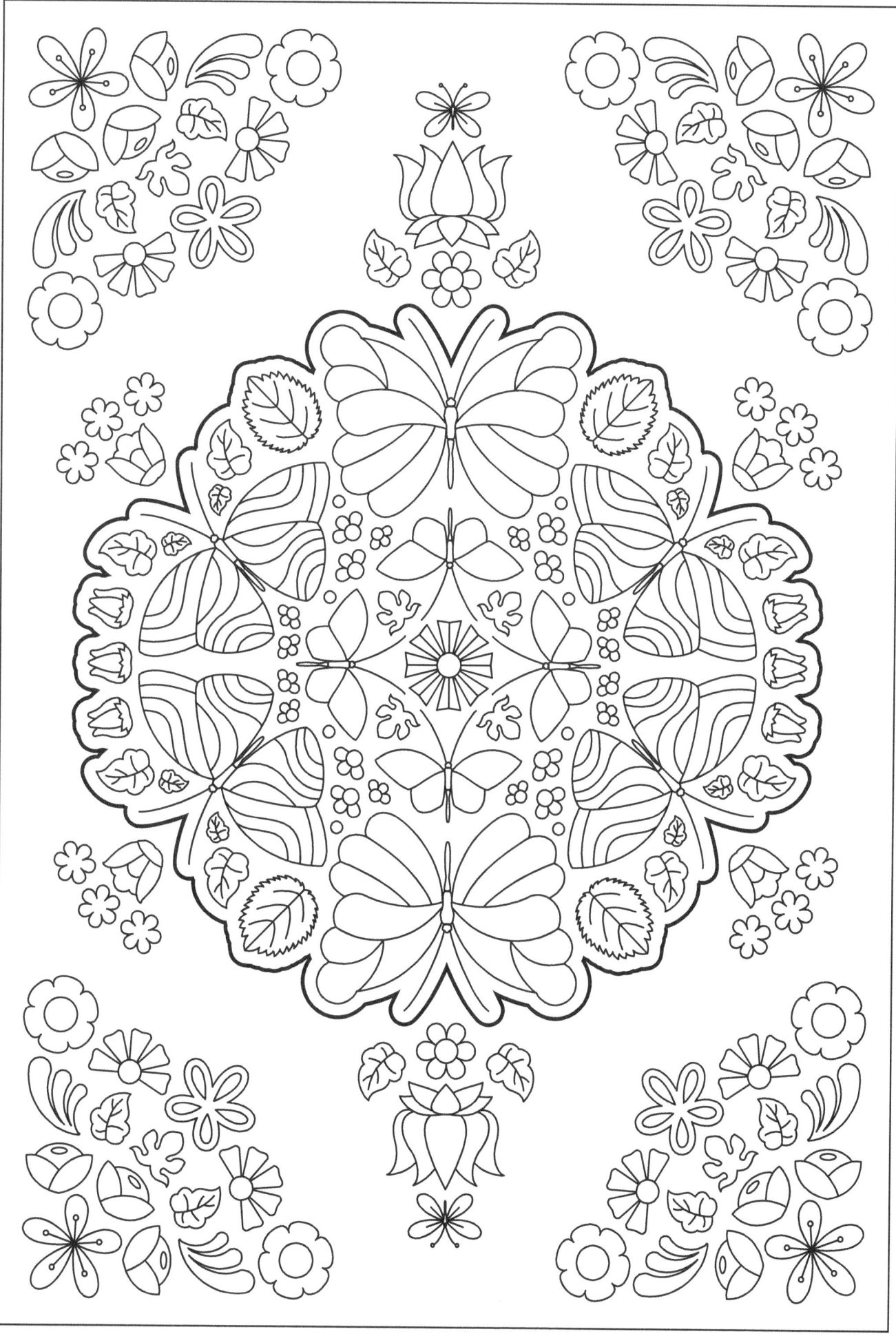

Floral Designs Coloring Book by TS Artworks

www.tsartworks.com

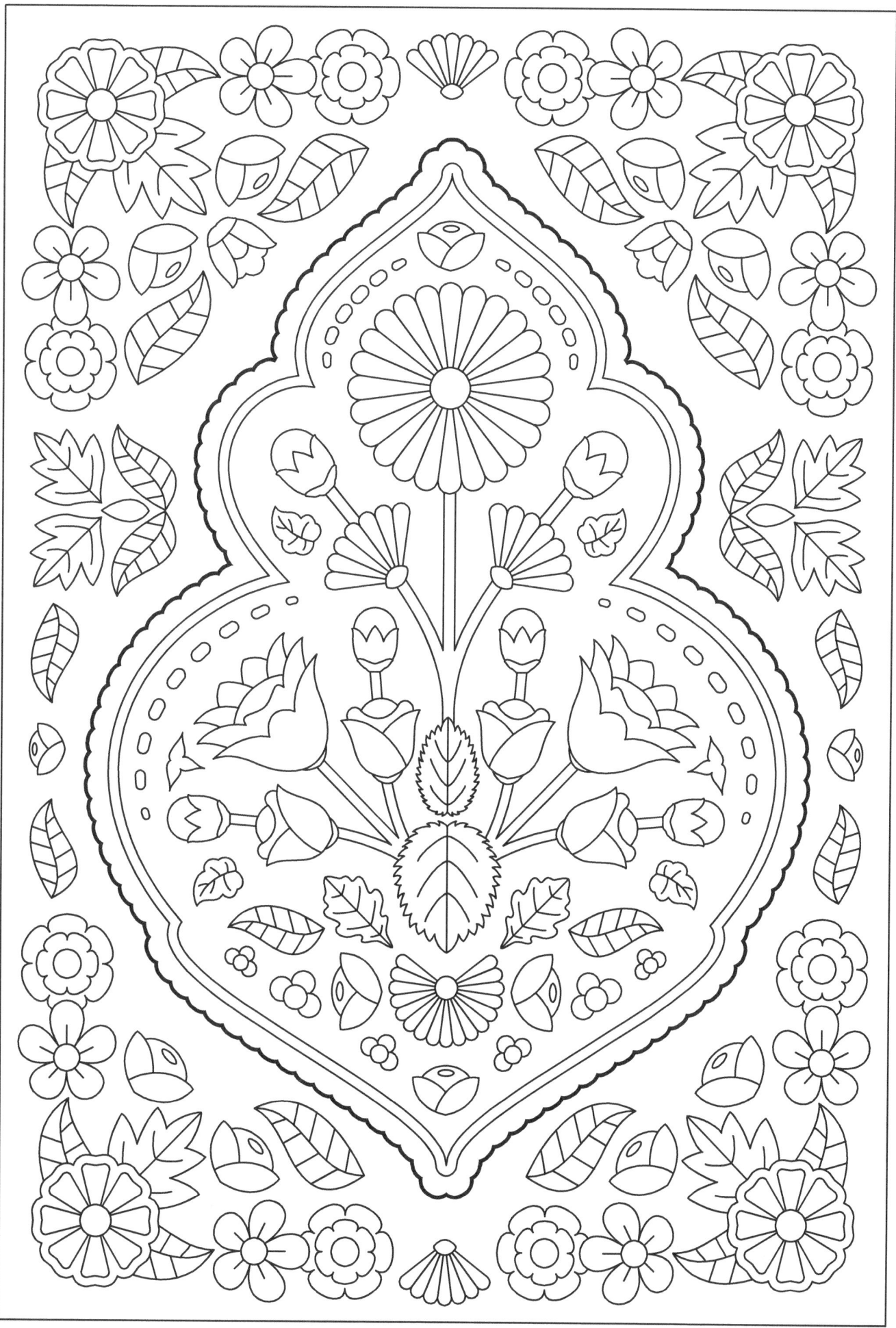

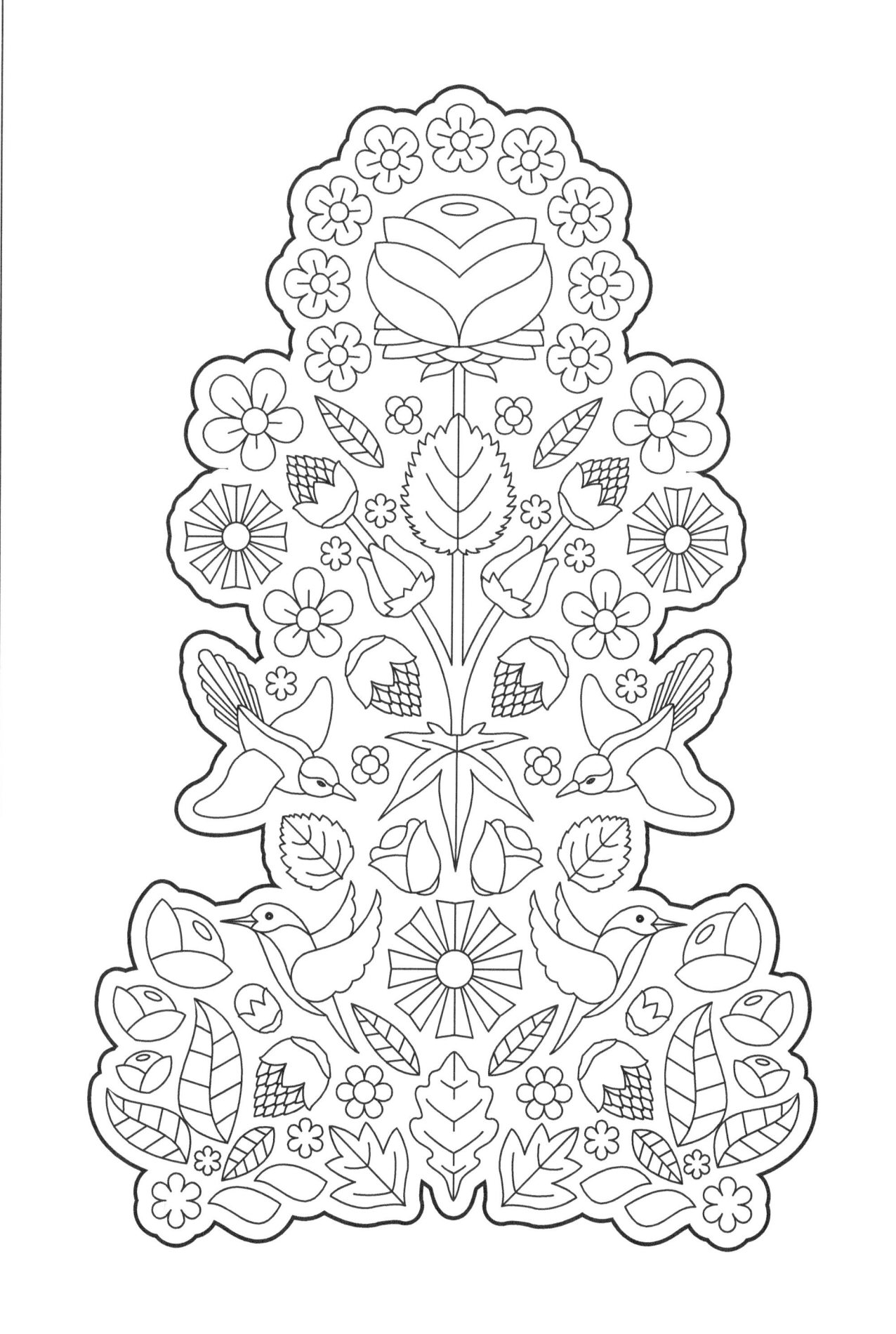

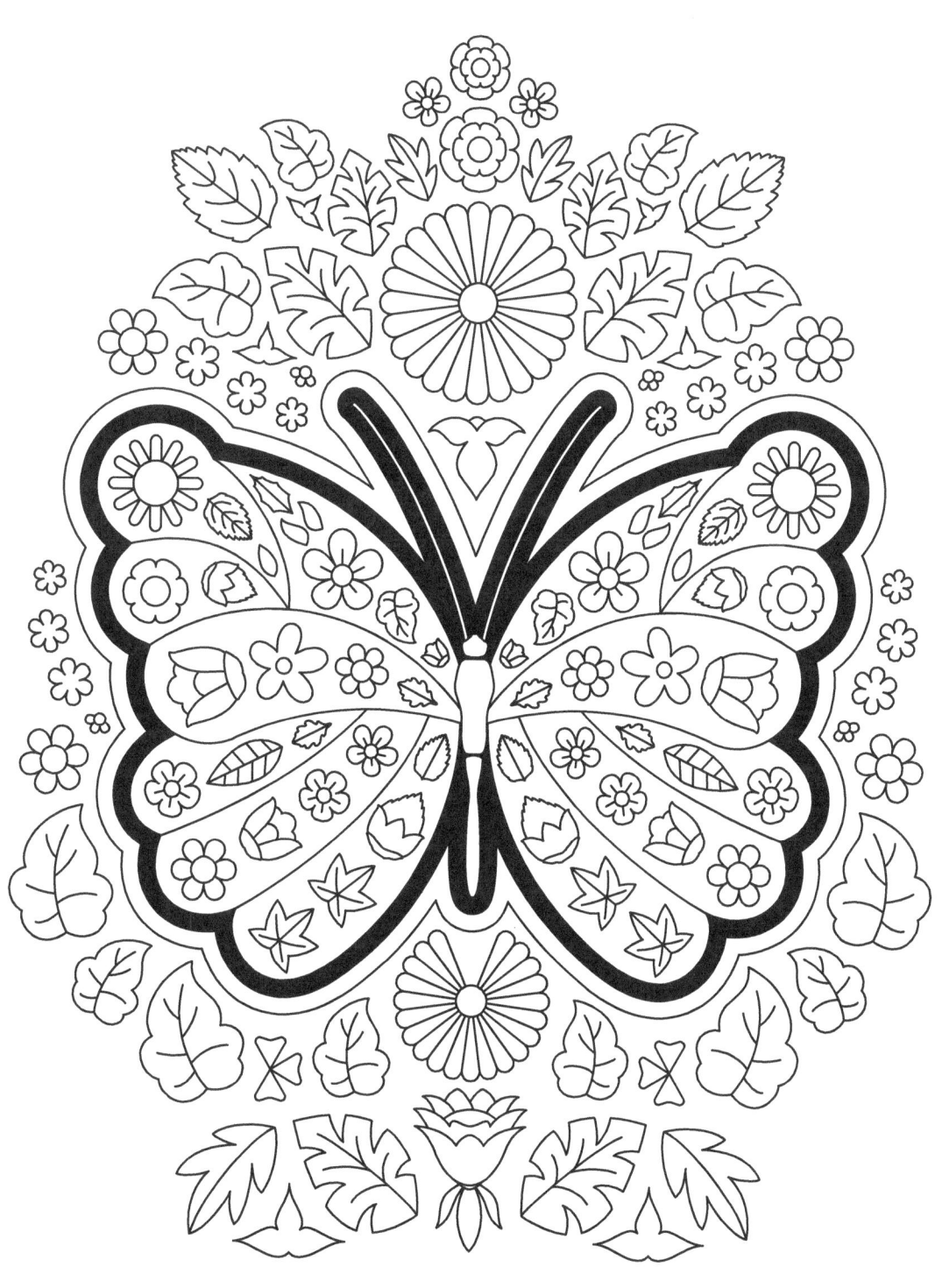

Floral Designs Coloring Book by TS Artworks

www.tsartworks.com

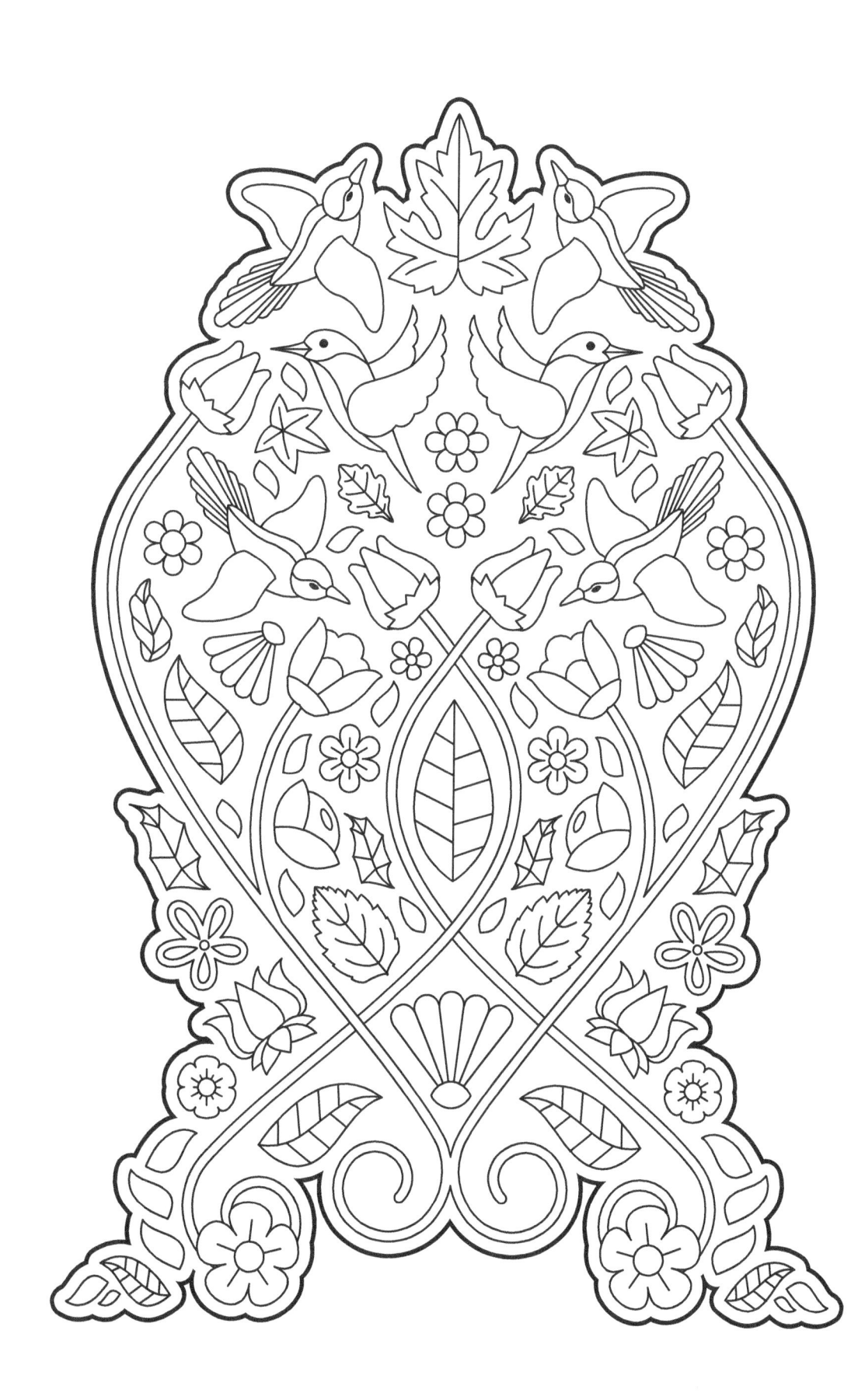

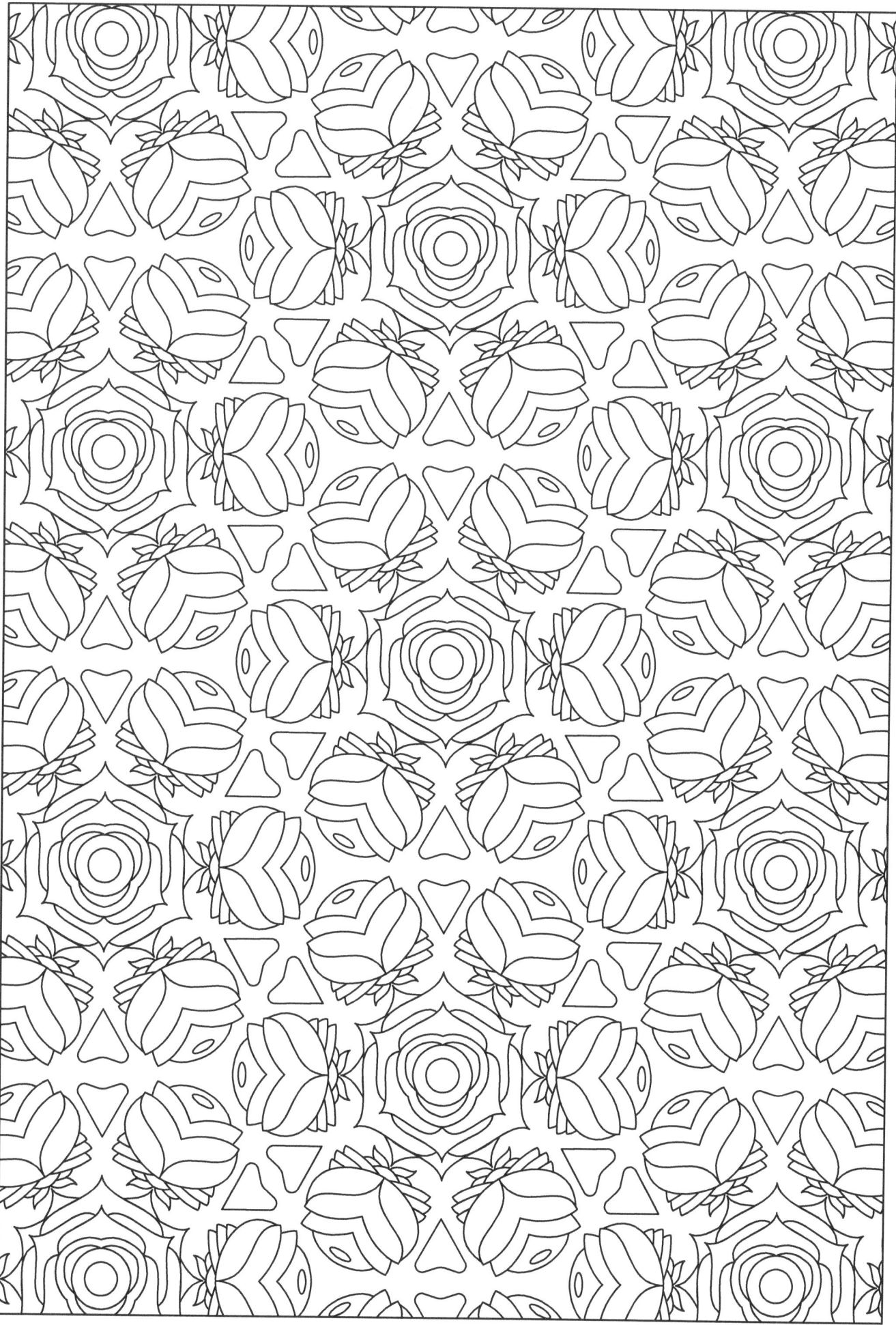

Floral Designs Coloring Book by TS Artworks

www.tsartworks.com

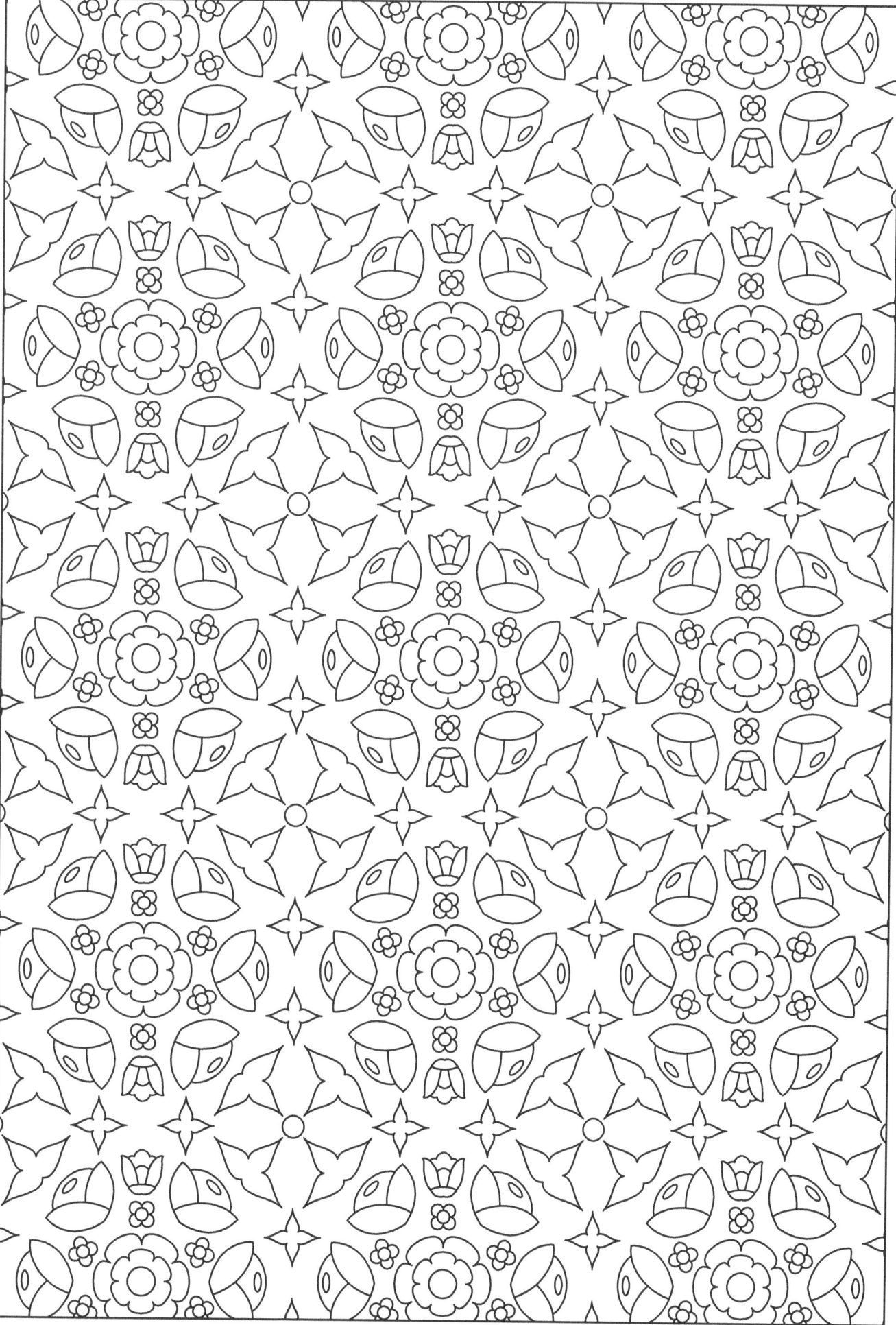

Floral Designs Coloring Book by TS Artworks

www.tsartworks.com

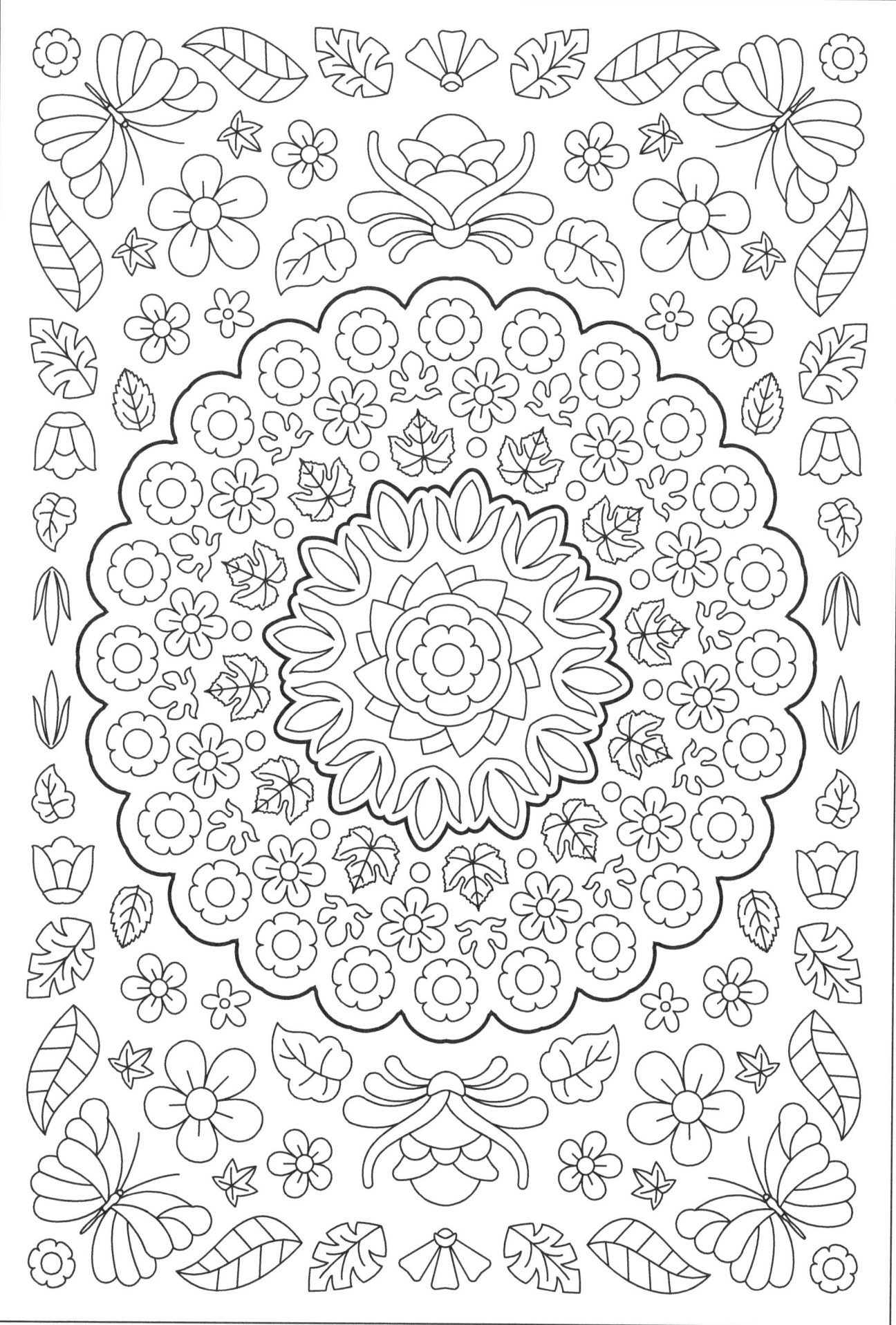

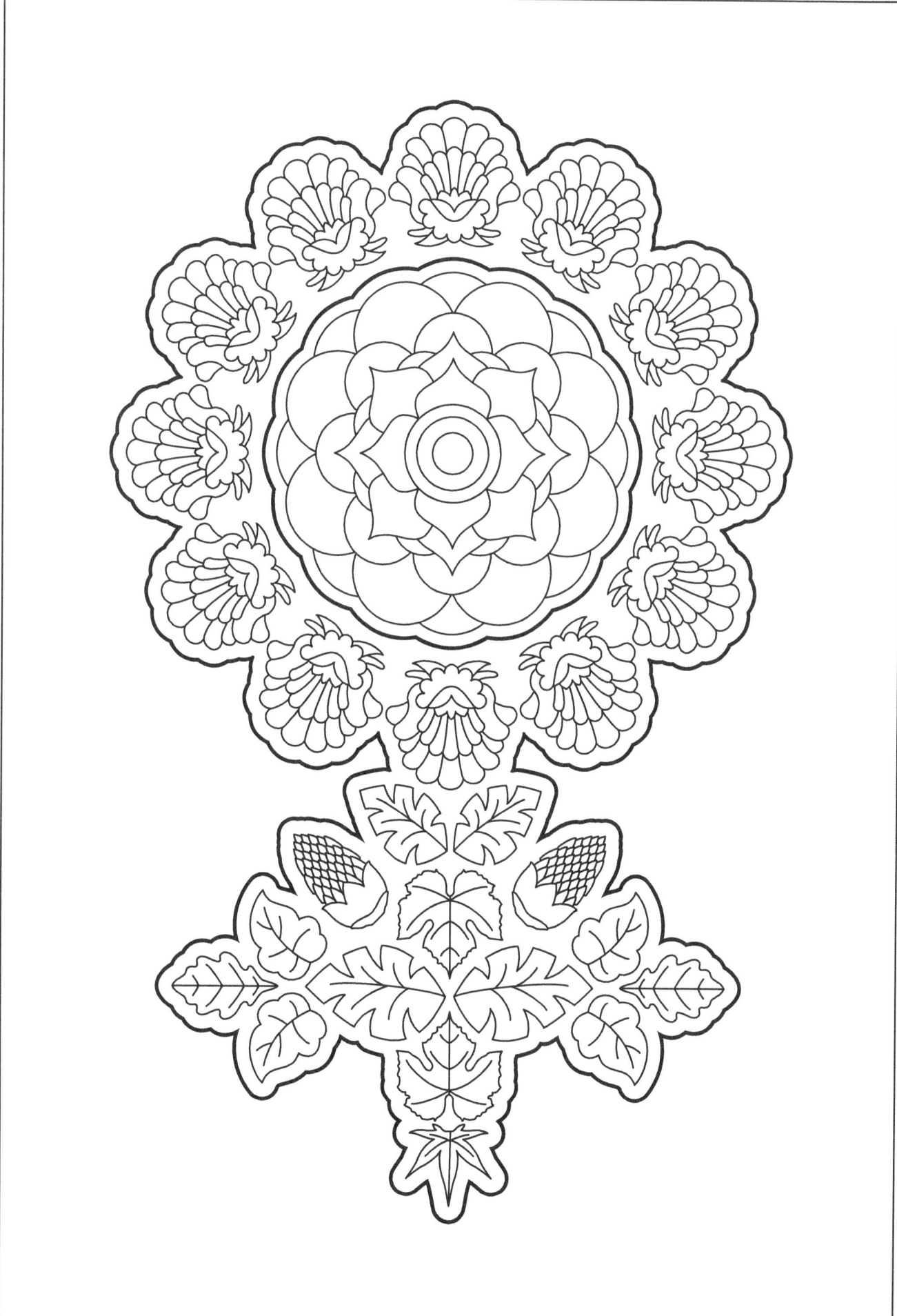

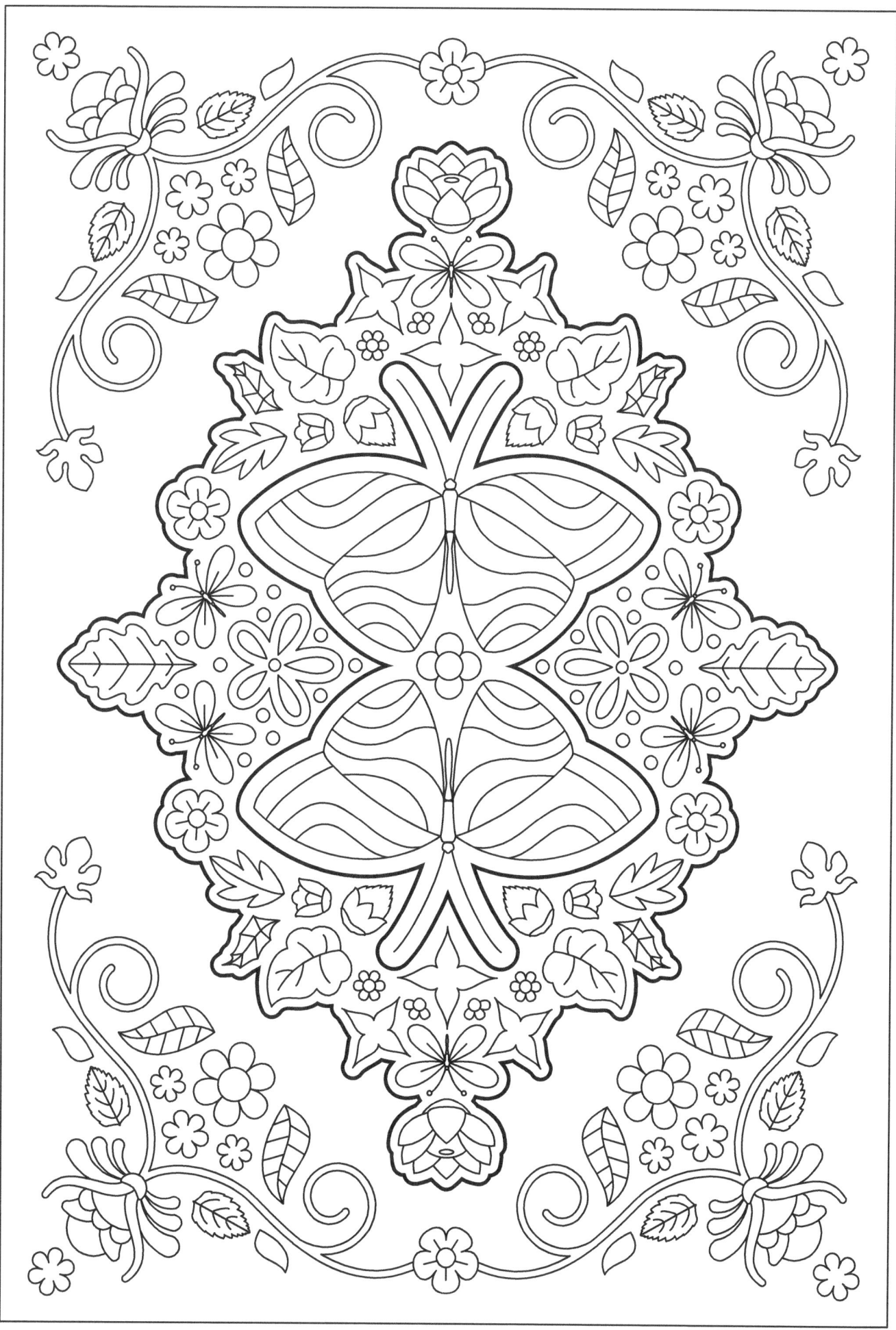

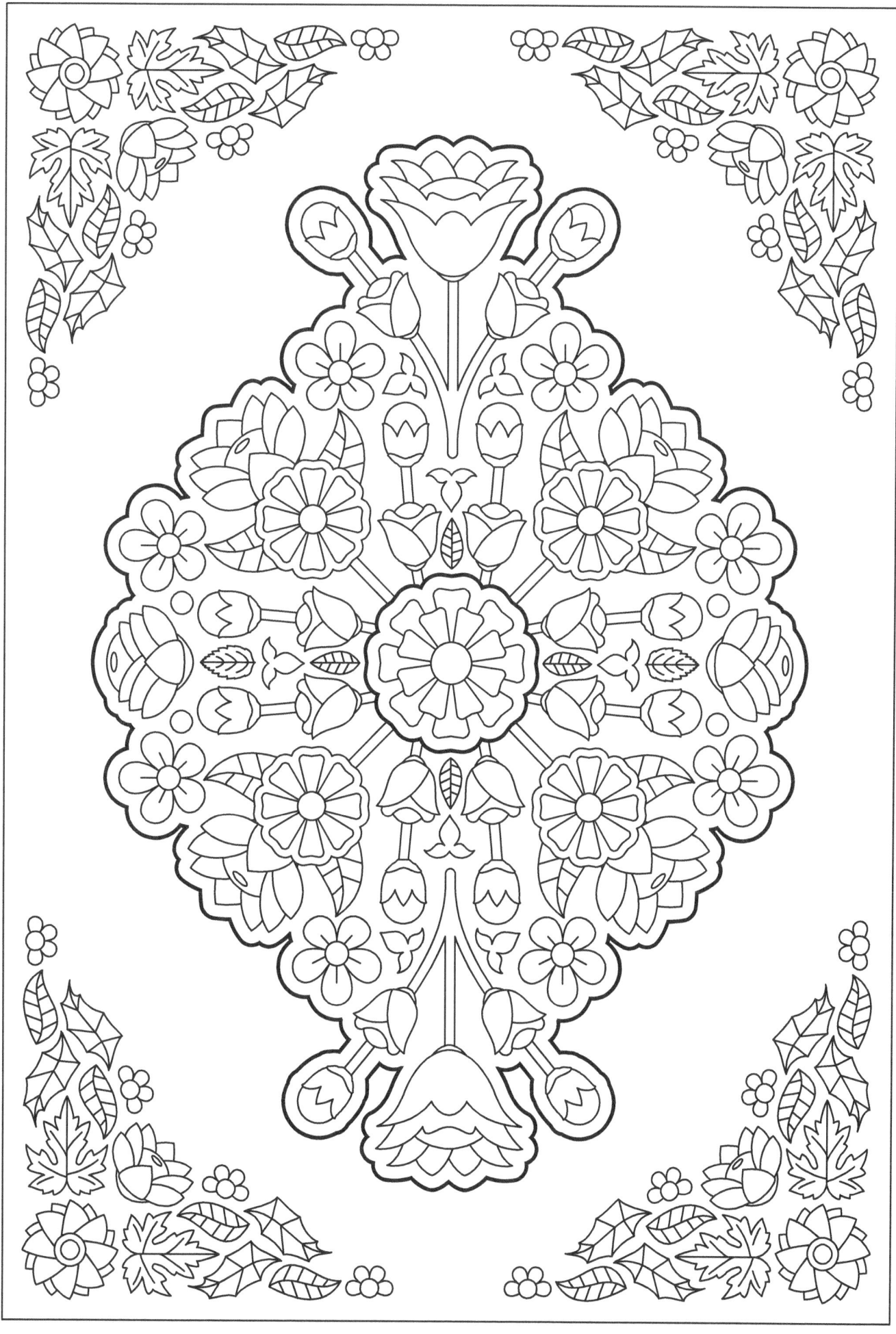

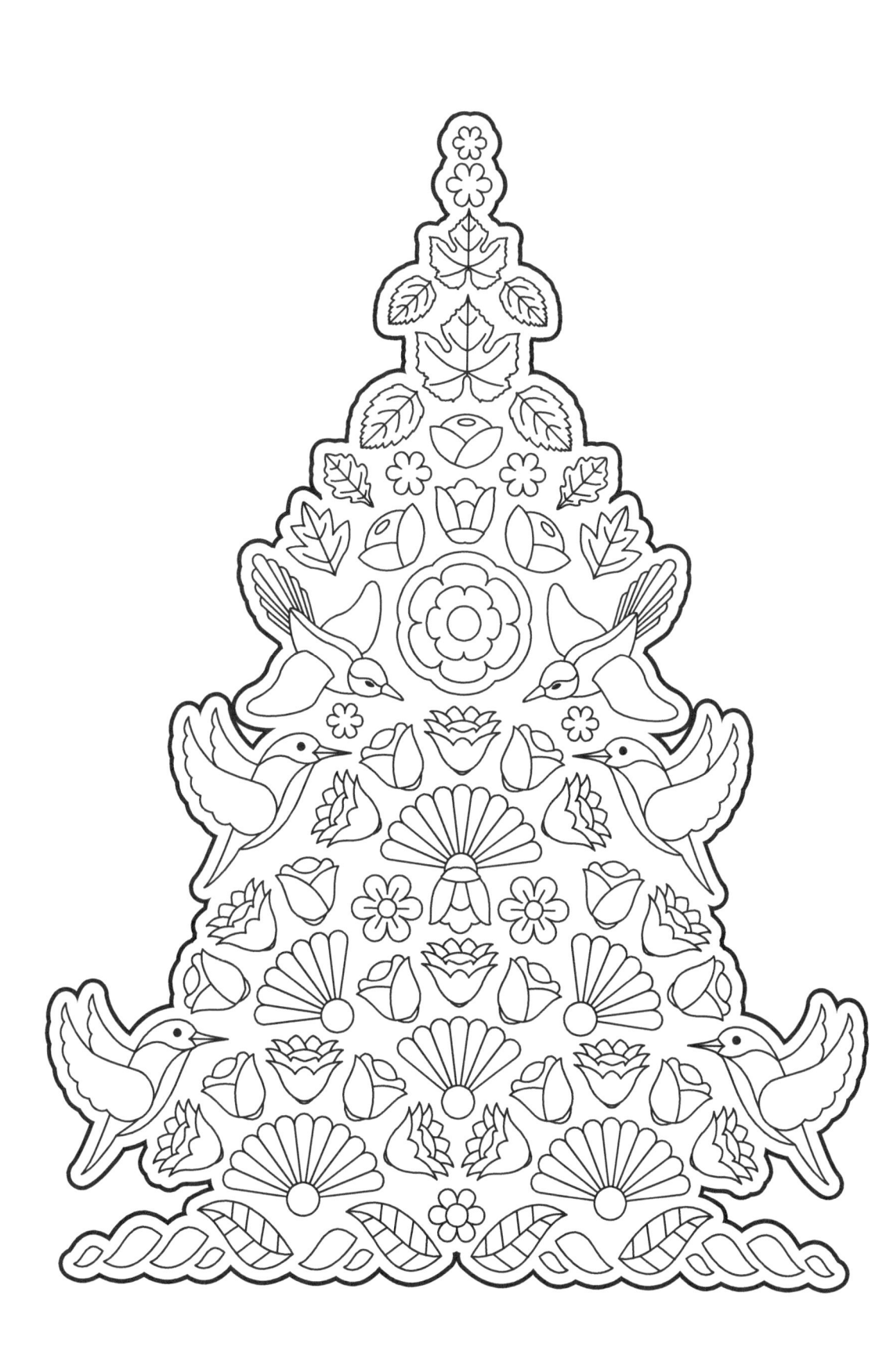

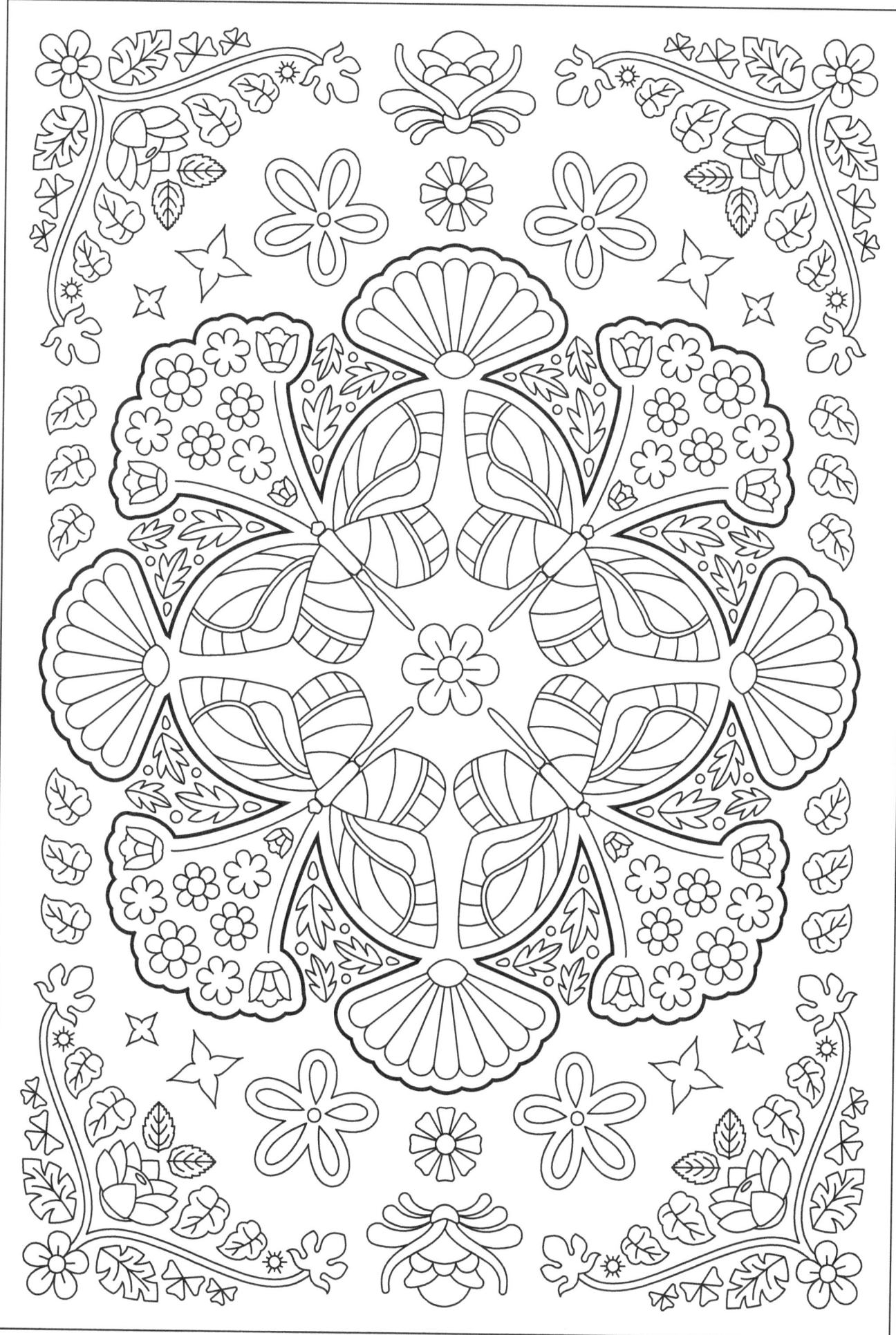

Floral Designs Coloring Book by TS Artworks

www.tsartworks.com

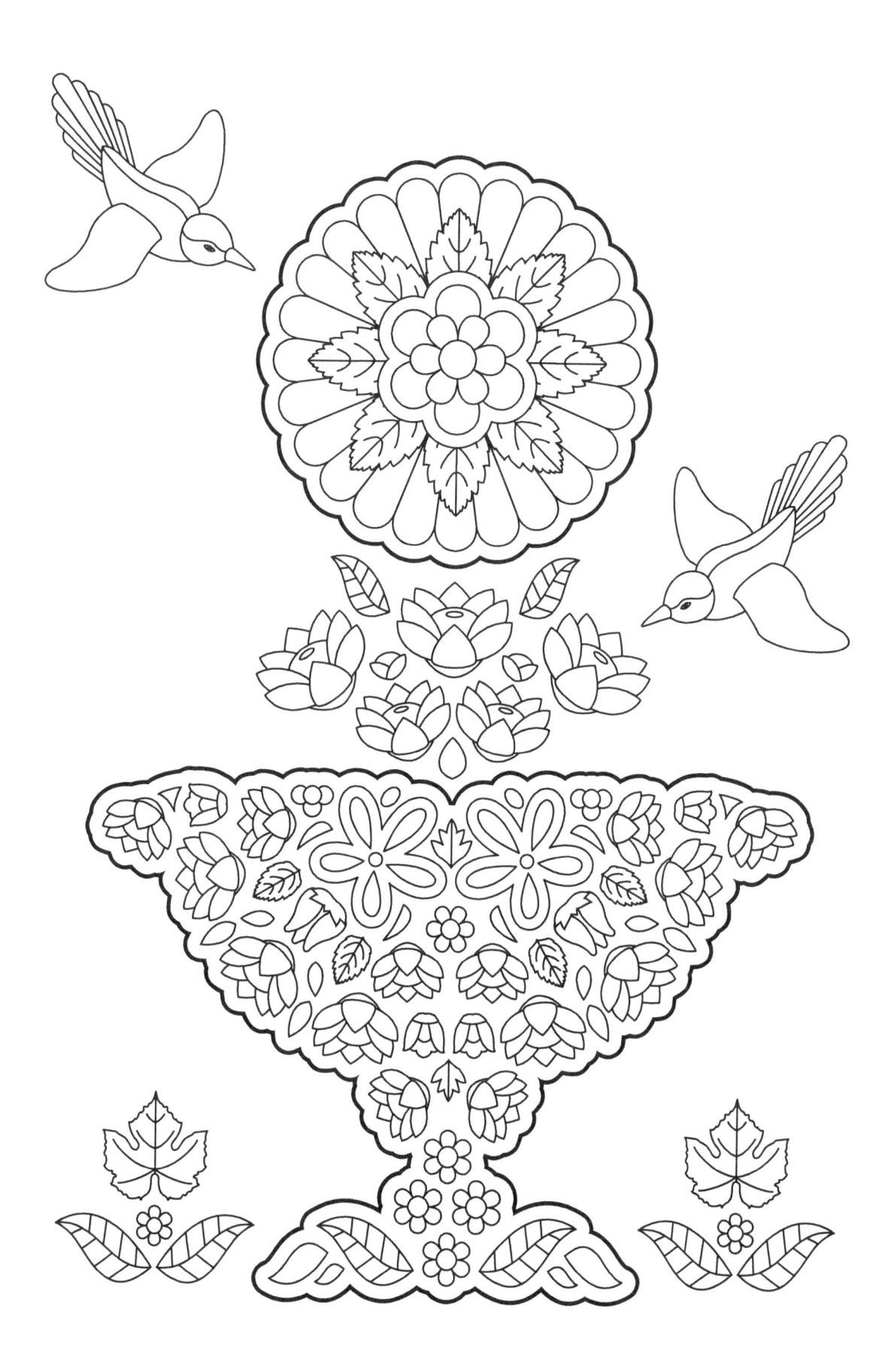

Floral Designs Coloring Book by TS Artworks

www.tsartworks.com

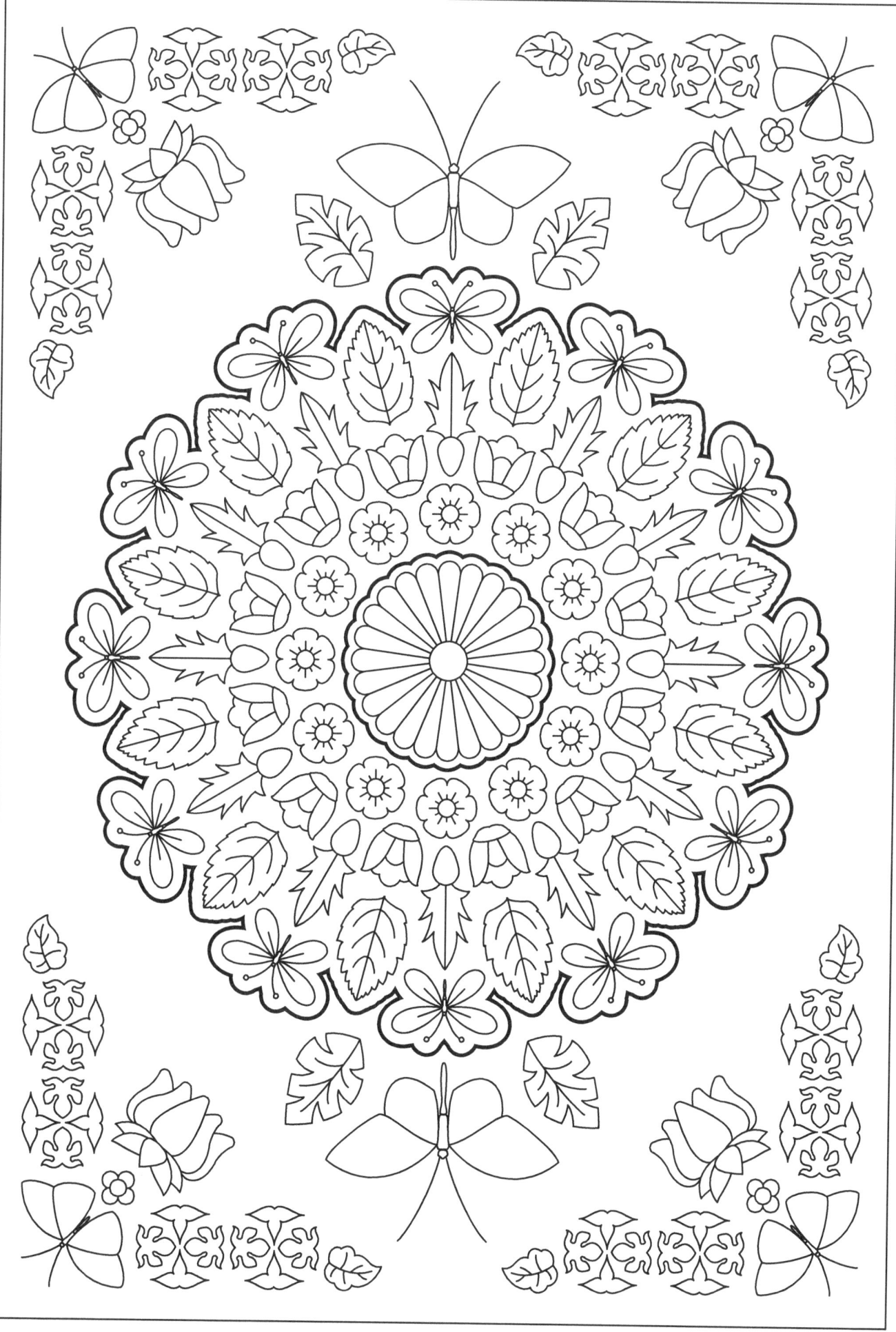

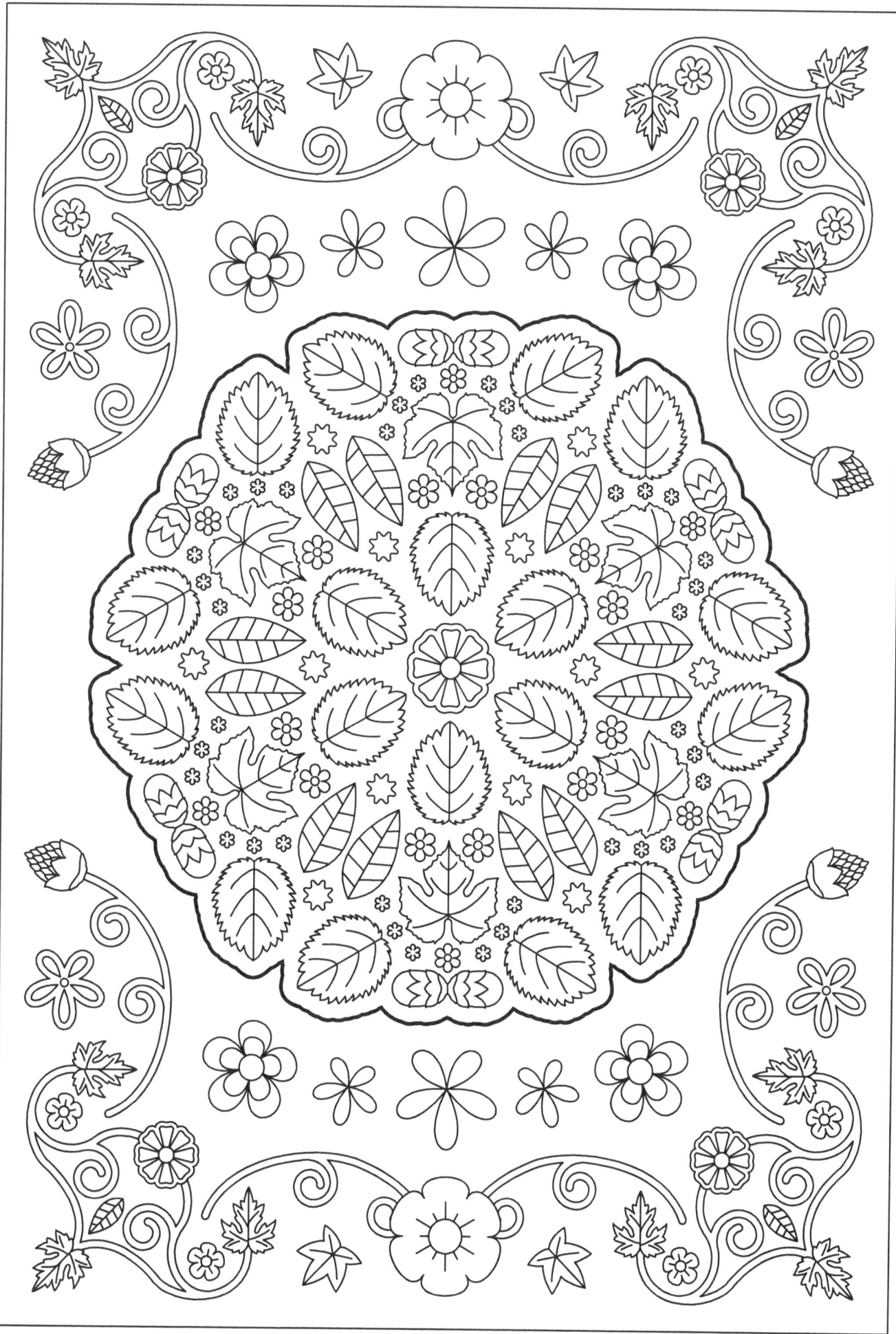

Floral Designs Coloring Book by TS Artworks

www.tsartworks.com

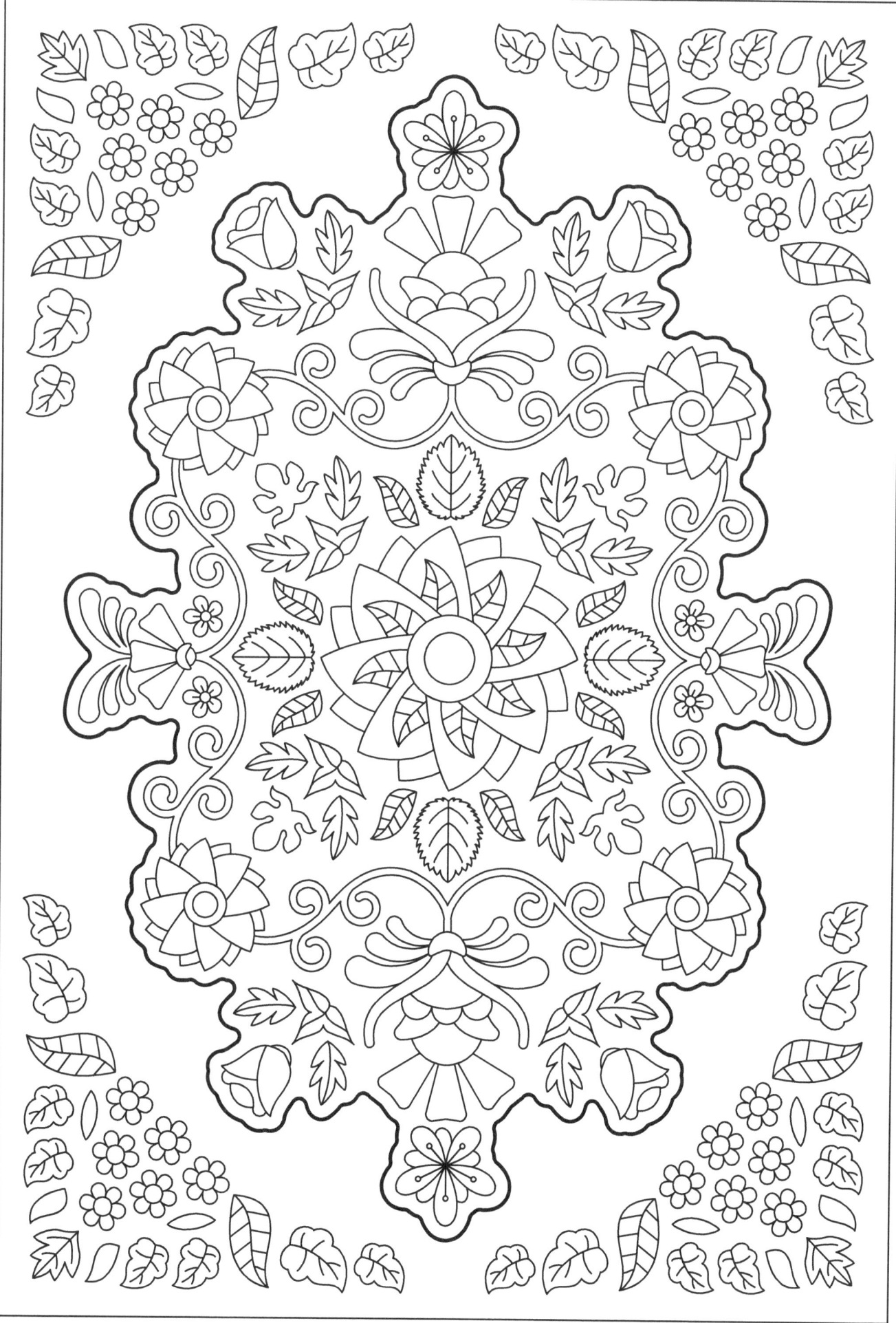

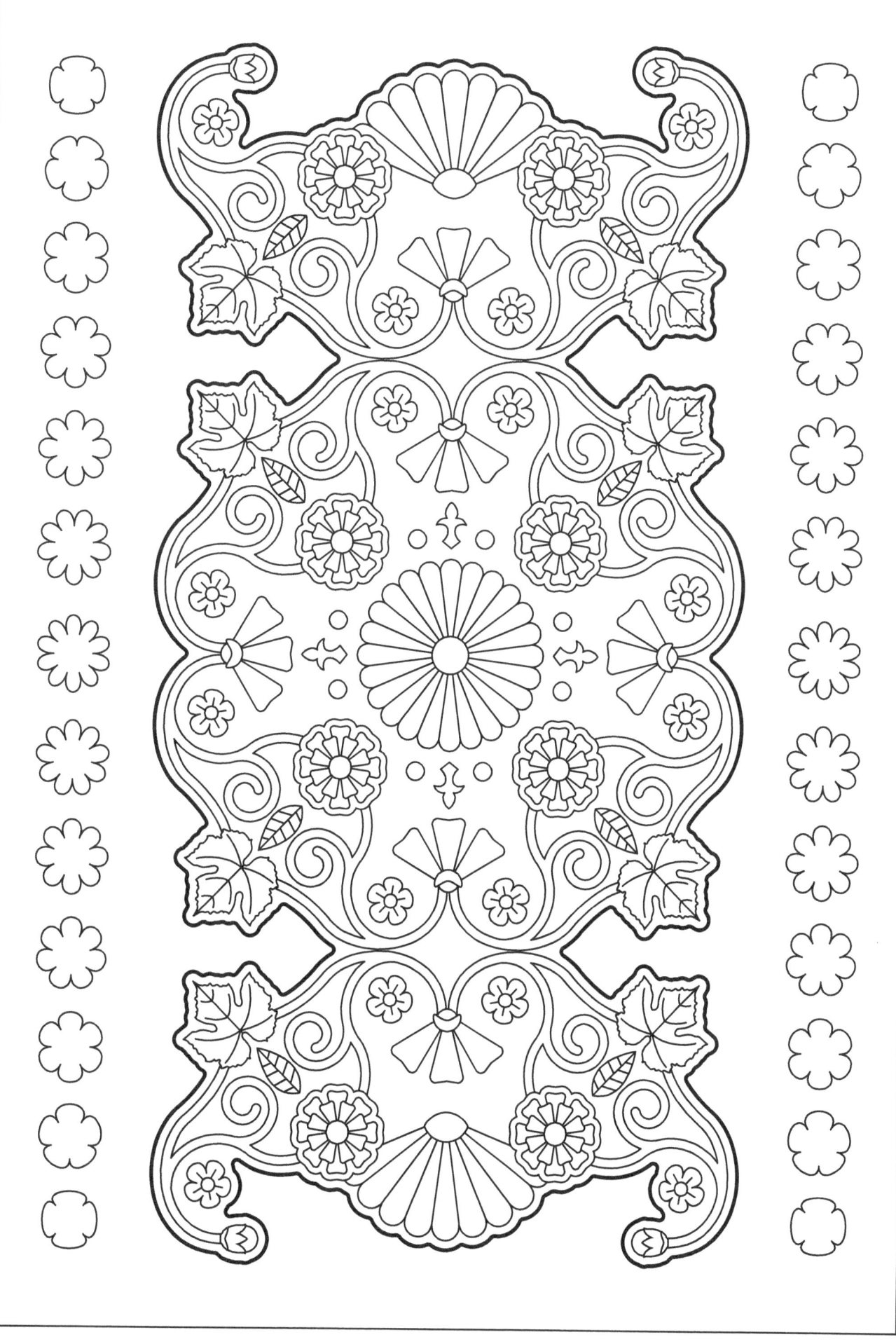

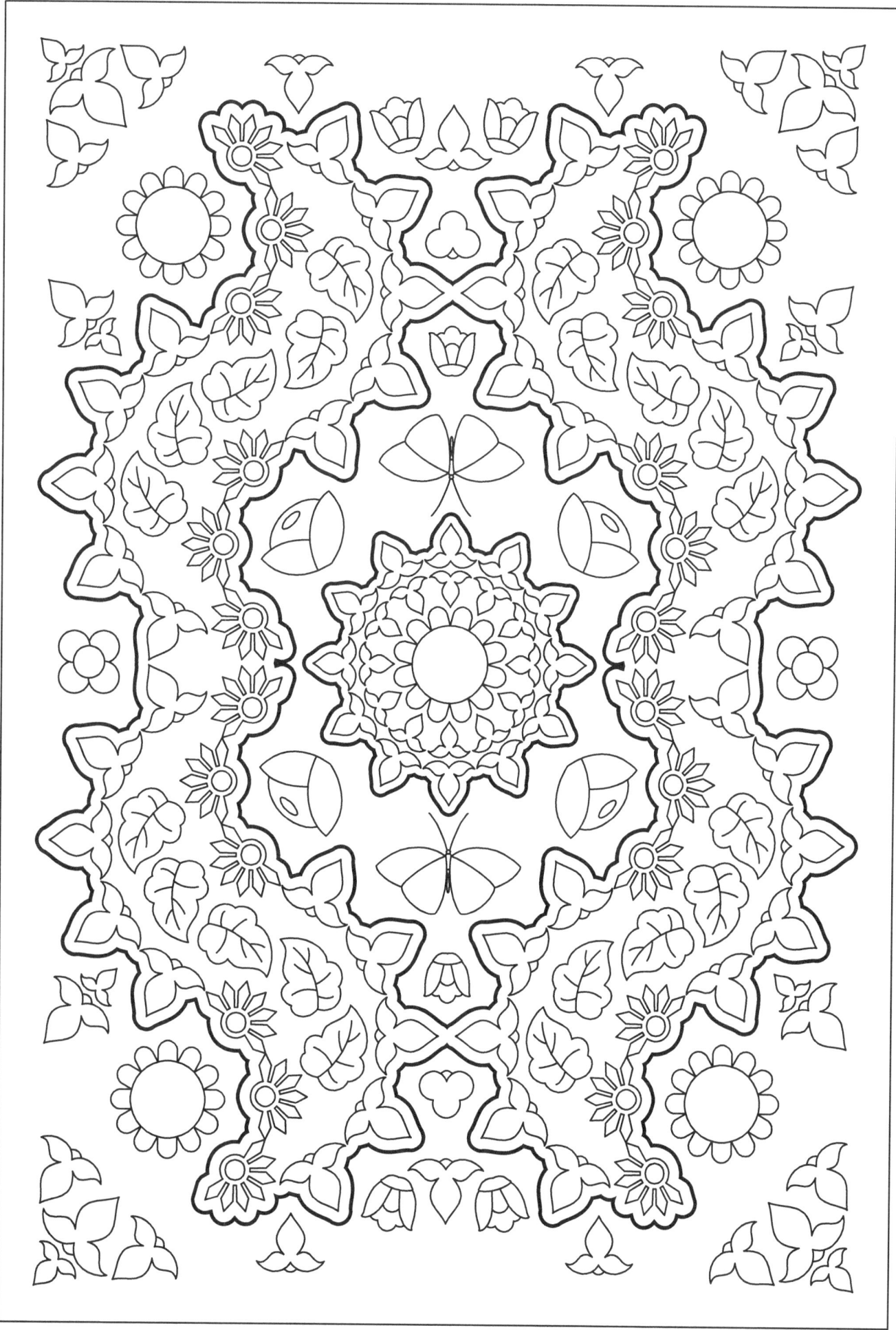

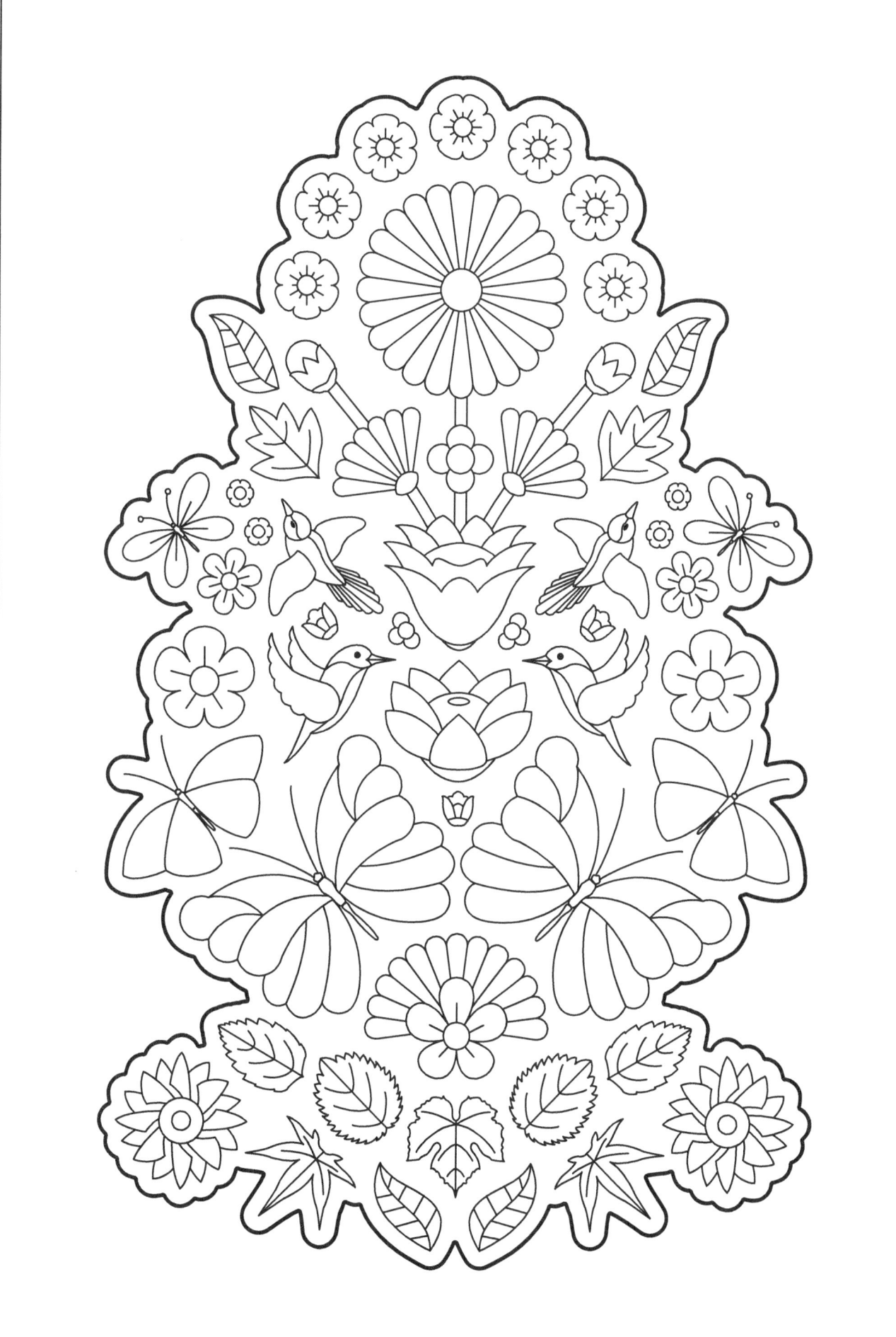

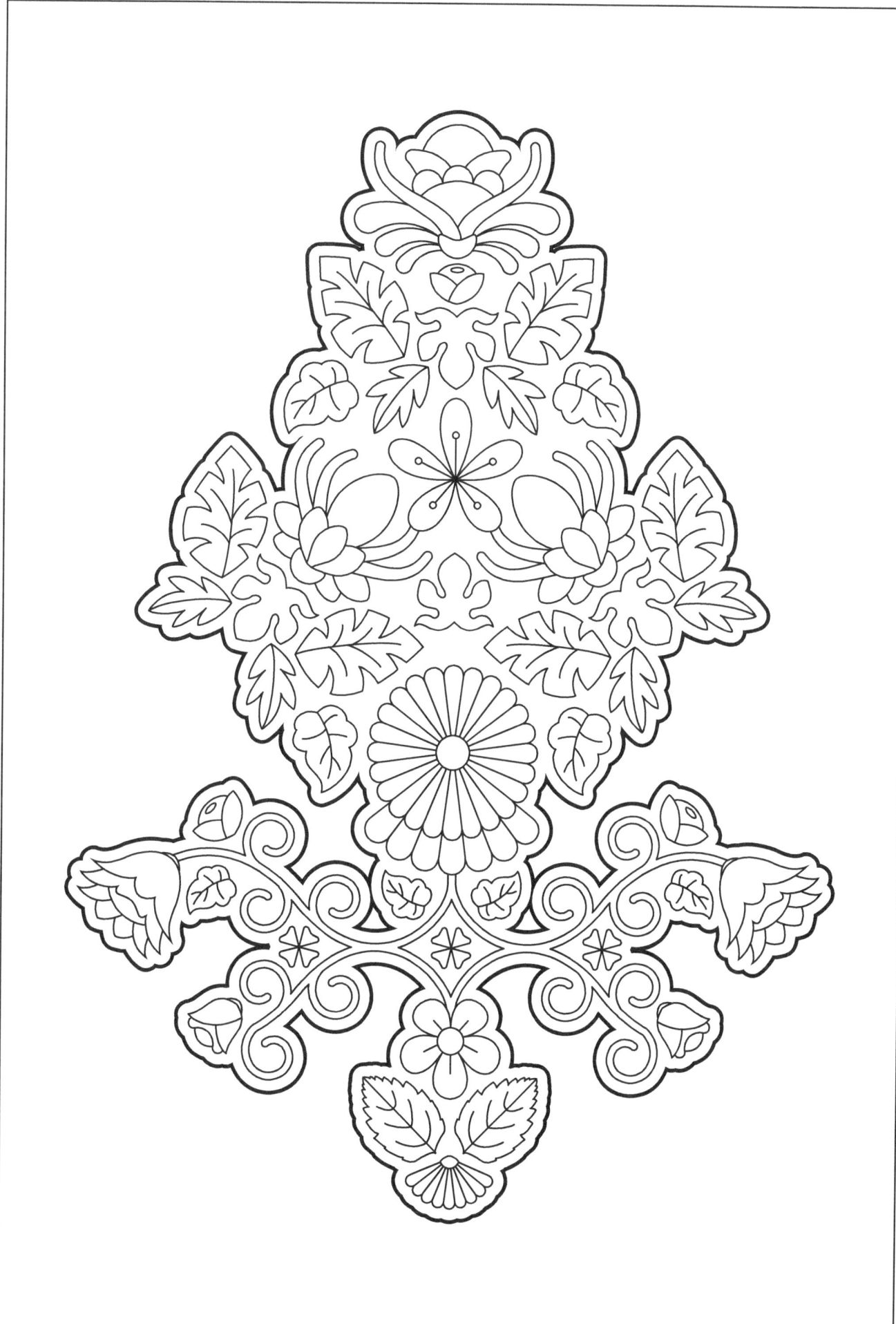

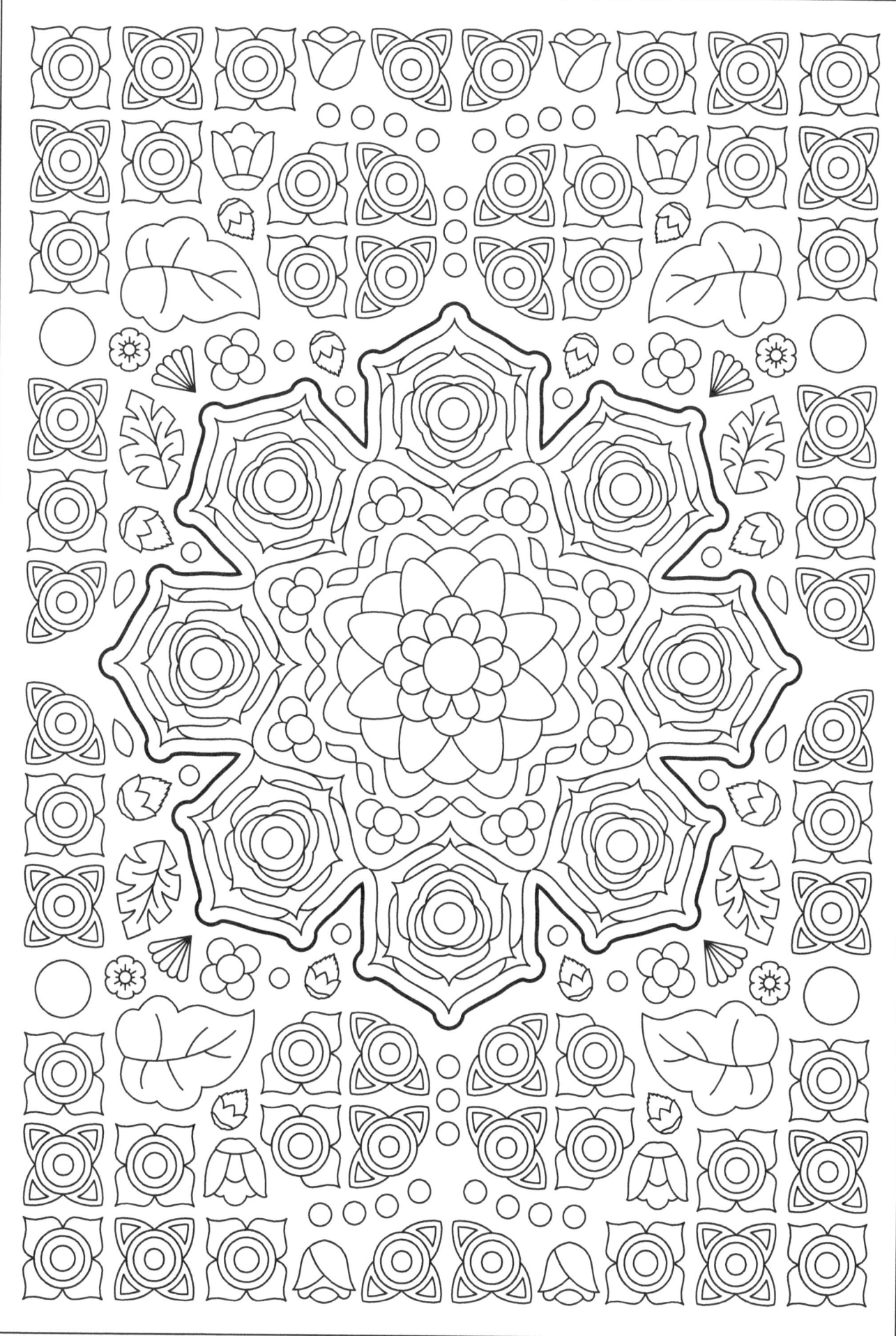

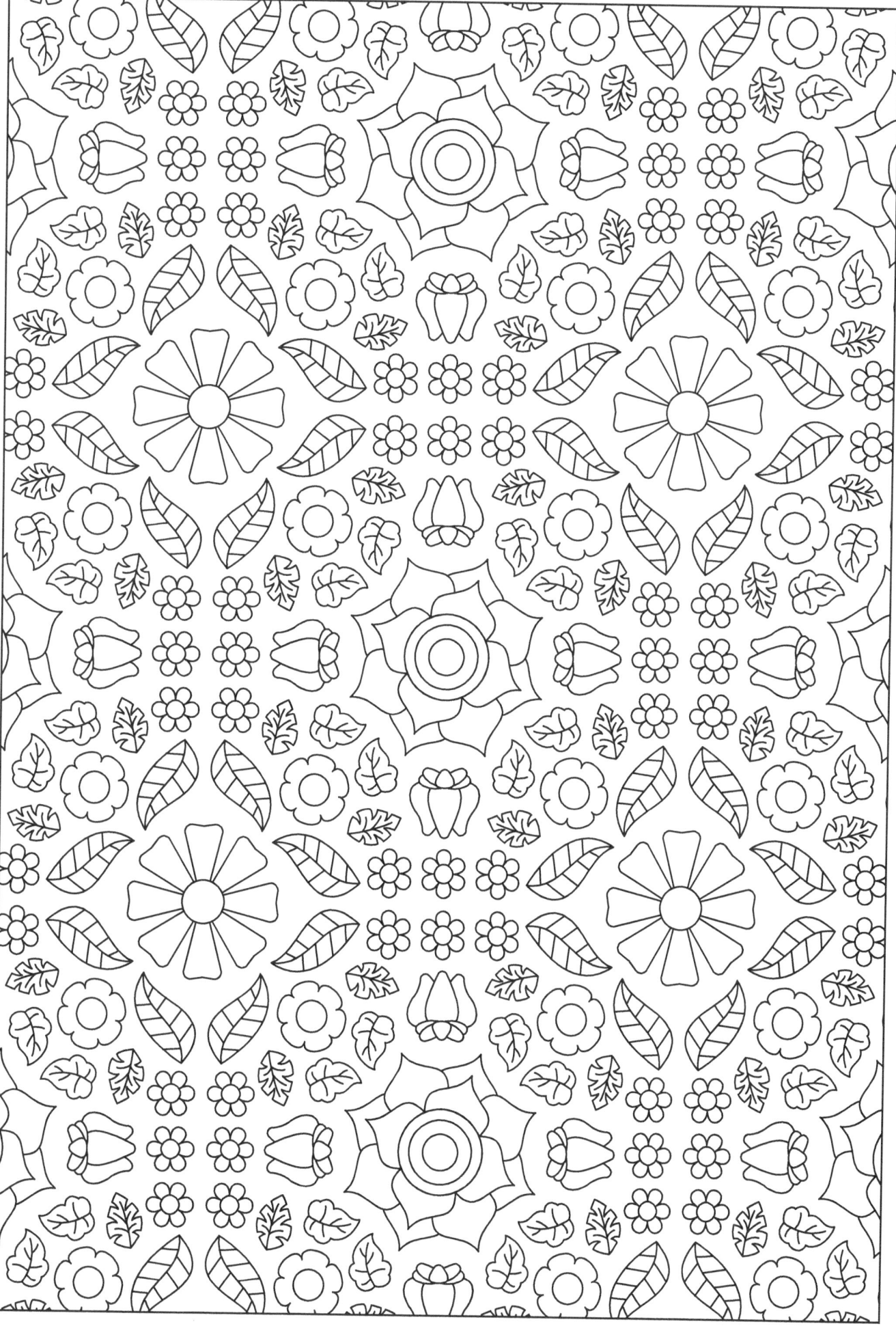

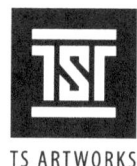

TS ARTWORKS

About the artist

TS Artworks is the creative space of Taranjit S Layal. After working for 20 plus years as an in-house designer for companies in India, Canada, and the US, Taranjit started his own creative practice in 2017. Influenced largely by symmetry, geometry, and technical art, he is on a quest of finding and developing his own visual voice and bringing it to life through his art, design, and illustration. Born and raised in India, he has been living and working in the US since 2003.

His goal as an artist and designer depends on the kind of project he is working on at a given time. It could be to decorate a surface, celebrate an occasion, uplift the soul, motivate the spirit, visualize an environment, represent an object, or convey information in a meaningful visual way. He loves variety in his work and strives to work on projects that have the potential of bringing some clarity, color, and cheer to our world.

You can buy products featuring his work from his online store at www.tsartworks.com. All of his work is also available for licensing. If you would like to license his work, please get in touch with him via his website.

This book is dedicated to the spirit of perseverance and steady persistence.
Thank you for buying this book! Color and enjoy!

---

www.tsartworks.com

www.ingramcontent.com/pod-product-compliance
Lightning Source LLC
Chambersburg PA
CBHW081018240526
45471CB00017B/3279